The Birth of a Transfer Society

THE BIRTH
OF A
TRANSFER SOCIETY

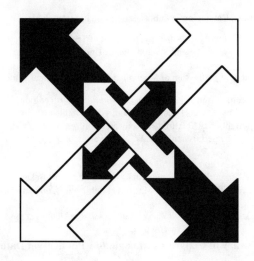

Terry L. Anderson
Peter J. Hill

Foreword by
James M. Buchanan

UNIVERSITY
PRESS OF
AMERICA

Lanham • New York • London

Copyright © 1989 by

University Press of America,® Inc.

4720 Boston Way
Lanham, MD 20706

3 Henrietta Street
London WC2E 8LU England

British Cataloging in Publication Information Available

Reprinted with permission of Macmillan Publishing Company, Inc.

Excerpts from *The American Constitution*, fourth edition,
by Alfred H. Kelly and Winfred A. Harbison.
Copyright © 1970 Alfred H. Kelly and Winfred A. Harbison.
Used by permission of W. W. Norton and Company, Inc.

Exceprts from *John Marshall: A Life in Law*,
by Leonard Baker. Copyright © 1974 by Leonard Baker.
Reprinted with permission of Macmillan Publishing Company, Inc.

Excerpts from *Social Theories of Jacksonian Democracy*,
edited by Joseph L. Blau, © 1954.

Library of Congress Cataloging-in-Publication Data

Anderson, Terry Lee, 1946–
The birth of a transfer society / Terry L. Anderson, Peter J. Hill.
p.   cm.
Reprint. Originally published: Stanford, Calif. : Hoover Institution Press,
Stanford University, ©1980. Originally published in series: Hoover
Press publication ; 229.
Includes bibliographical references.
1. Transfer payments—United States—History.   2. Income distribution—
United States—History.   3. Right of property—United States—History.
4. Industry and state—United States—History.   I. Hill, Peter J.   II. Title.
HC110.I5A72   1989   339.5'2'0973—dc20   89–16713 CIP

ISBN 0–8191–7563–3

To Janet and Lois

Contents

Tables

Foreword

How did we get here from there?

In this challenging monograph, Terry Anderson and Peter Hill tell us how shifts in the conception of politics and government got us into the mess we are in. But they do more; they tell us just about when it happened. American public philosophy, reflected in ideas about legal-political order, became confused roughly a century ago. The New Deal and its progenies were not new at all.

The Founding Fathers had the wisdom to know that governments have a natural proclivity to get out of hand. They sought to keep the state productive by the imposition of severe constitutional limits. The people were conceived to create governments as means of securing collectively what could not readily be secured privately. Governments were not conceived as furthering any "public interest" independent of the people to whom they owed their very creation.

The basic conception changed dramatically in the late nineteenth century. Governments' alleged pursuit of the public interest justified the initiation of transfer activity motivated by changing legal ideologies and newly dominant political coalitions. The whole complex of institutions and agencies that we call government came to be recognized as a source of transfer profits or rents. The predictable result was that rent seekers came to invest increasingly in transfer activity through politics and less in productive activity through politics or the market. Zero- and negative-sum games replaced positive-sum games, and as yet the shift shows no signs of being complete.

The story is an old one, and a sad one. But rules that were changed for the worse because of shifts in ideas can be changed for the better because of changes in ideas. Anderson and Hill properly concentrate on the relevance and importance of the constitutional structure. They explain just how the old rules, partly implicit, broke down. They recognize that there is little scope for improvement within existing rules. They join the call for a constitutional revolution.

Ideas change slowly and unpredictably. We may hope that America is now in the process of generating the set of ideas required for the new public philosophy that will make such a constitutional revolution a reality of the next century.

JAMES M. BUCHANAN

Preface

If economists have anything to offer society, it is a way of thinking. This particular book illustrates a way of thinking about how individuals acting alone or in groups increase their control over resources, that is, their wealth. Although we are economists and do draw heavily on legal history, this work is not intended solely for those conversant with these areas of study. We have attempted to write with a minimum of economic jargon so that our way of thinking will be understandable and useful to all readers. For the economist and the legal historian, however, a caveat is in order. We do not claim to have made any major breakthroughs in economic theory or any startling discoveries of new evidence. Hence the professional economist desiring technical, theoretical discussions regarding the first- and second-order conditions for wealth maximization will be disappointed. To that economist we do offer an application that provides insight into the present structure of the economy. Similarly the legal scholar seeking new interpretations of important cases or the unearthing of precedents leading to path-breaking legal decisions will find not them, but a way of thinking about legal history and the impact of that history.

We do claim to have developed a taxonomy that aids our understanding of how individuals in the United States have altered their efforts to increase wealth. Institutions, or rules of the game, are important determinants of behavior, and the history of these rules in the United States is central to our study. Our analysis provides a framework for organizing interpretations of the Constitution and the impact of these on behavior. We make no pretense of offering a complete explanation for the changes in institutions, but we do examine some variables that have influenced this process.

Our goals in developing this analytical framework and in presenting the historical evidence are threefold: (1) to provide historical insights into the reasons for the increase in governmental influence on the distribution of wealth; (2) to stimulate the reader to apply the productive/transfer dichotomy we develop to everyday actions; and (3), and perhaps most important, to influence ideas. The true test of this book will be whether the ideas we develop have any impact on the organization of society. Ideas greatly influenced the American Revolution and the ensuing Constitution; they helped shape the nature of our democracy during the antebellum period; and they affected the rise of governmental regulation during the late nineteenth century. Rules governing behavior have always been and will always be subject to interpretation, which is in turn a product of ideology. If we are to reduce the number of negative-sum games played in our society, a revolution in ideas is necessary. We hope that this book will be a part of that revolution.

One final caveat about our work is in order. In researching and writing *The Birth of a Transfer Society*, we initially assumed that we were operating in the standard, neoclassical economics paradigm where only positive statements were made. We still believe that efficiency standards are useful in judging various economic outcomes but now recognize that writing a historical work requires, at several points, the use of implicit standards of legitimacy. Three examples illustrate this point. First, in examining the Constitution, we implicitly assume that most rights established there are legitimate. Second, as we point out in chapter 2, our entire discussion of transfers representing net social waste assumes that bureaucrats have no legitimate claim to any utility received in the transfer process. And third, in our discussion of slavery we recognize that certain transfers can be justified to rectify previously illegitimate holdings. We are not presenting a theory of justice, but the reader should be aware that this work makes some basic assumptions regarding rights, particularly the integrity of the individual and the right to freedom from coercion except as implied by the social contract. We believe that these assumptions are not revolutionary and that similar legitimacy criteria are implicit in most other economic and historical analyses. However, we find forthright specification of our position desirable.

We are grateful for help from numerous individuals in generating this work. Since our research has developed over several years, it is very difficult to recall all those responsible for providing useful ideas and insights. There are a few, however, whose influence and assistance have been so obvious that even our short memories have not forgotten them. First, we are indebted to James Buchanan for his thinking and writing, which formed the foundation on which we built. His insight and perspective have been invaluable, and we are grateful for his Foreword to this work. Douglass North's work has also provided important building blocks. Ernst R. Habicht, Jr., Robert Hessen, Paul Heyne, Jonathan R. T. Hughes, Alvin Rabushka, and Dan Usher read the manuscript at various stages and offered detailed suggestions. Mary Whittinghill provided valuable research assistance, and John Ziemer greatly improved the manuscript with his editing. Our failure to follow some of those suggestions or address issues they raised reflects more on our judgment than theirs. Finally, we thank the National Fellows Program of the Hoover Institution on War, Revolution and Peace for its financial support for Terry Anderson in 1977–78 and the Center for Libertarian Studies for a fellowship in 1979 that allowed completion of the manuscript.

ONE

⟷

Games People Play

Most economic analysis begins with the premise that an individual attempts to maximize his own well-being. The present analysis is no exception—allowing every individual to pursue this objective is one of the goals of a free society. The important question that always arises, however, is the proper extent of this freedom. If anarchy is not to prevail, collective choices regarding which individual actions are to be encouraged and which discouraged must be made. This book presents one taxonomy for making this choice. In order to understand this taxonomy, let us consider several scenarios depicting individuals or groups pursuing different means of increasing their well-being.

The Ohio River Valley, 1840: Harlan Stipes steps from his log farmhouse and begins the chores around his farmstead. After finishing, he plans to begin seeding his wheat crop for this year. Last night at dusk he finished his plowing and harrowing, pushing his horses harder than usual because he knew that today they would have a day of rest. Wheat is Stipes's main cash crop. If he gets a substantial yield, he will have enough cash income to purchase not only the necessities for another year of farming, but also a few luxuries for himself, his wife, and his three children.

Pittsburgh, Pennsylvania, 1870: In a densely populated district in the city, where many recent immigrants reside, Manny Franks descends a staircase from his rather dilapidated second-floor apartment and walks to the local butcher shop. The butcher, a man for whom he has done several favors, has been saving meat scraps for him all week. The butcher wraps the scraps carefully in a piece of brown paper, ties it with string, and hands it to Manny, who returns to his apartment. In a dark corner of the room, behind cages of wood and metal scraps, two bull terriers, or pit bulls, are sleeping. He carefully divides the meat between the terriers, pets them for a while, and contemplates their next engagement. Although sporadically employed in Pittsburgh's steel mills, Manny's major function in life is training, fighting, and selling dogs for pit fighting, a popular sport among both the rich and the poor of the city. As evidenced by the scars, one of Manny's dogs is an old hand at this sort of fighting. The other dog has yet to engage a serious foe in the pit but has tasted blood in several training bouts with nonfighting dogs. In a good bout Manny can make $120, a handsome sum for the time.

New York City, 1892: John Sampson sits in his well-furnished office carefully going over a long list of tables prepared for him by his accountant. Mr. Sampson, an executive officer with a major railroad, is pleased with the results shown in the tables. He is slated to appear before the Interstate Commerce Commission later in the week and wants to argue that rate stabilization is a necessary condition for the long-run health of the industry. His tables show quite conclusively, he thinks, that such stabilization would prevent the cutthroat, predatory competition that has worked to the disadvantage of his company. To ensure a favorable decision he will argue that competition may harm consumers, although he knows that the decision will eventually result in higher transportation costs.

Butte, Montana, 1954: Bill Tawns, secretary of the Painters Union, is concerned about the rapid increase of air compressors and spray guns on outside painting jobs, particularly on large construction projects. Several union members have recently complained to him about other union members' using the new technology and underbidding them on some jobs. Tawns hurriedly drafts an amendment to the union's work rules outlawing the use of the new equipment. He plans to present the amendment at a union meeting that night. He has little doubt that if passed it will be enforced, for Butte is a strong union town, and no worker or supplier would think of crossing a picket line. The result, of course, will be higher painting prices.

Des Moines, Iowa, 1975: Emily Whiteside, lawyer for the Akona Plastics Corporation, carefully examines last year's tax code. She will attend a convention of the industry trade association next week and wants to know the precise effect of proposed tax changes on her firm. Her intention is to prepare a carefully written brief for the association lobbyist, who will follow quite closely the testimony before the appropriate legislative subcommittees. She expects that almost 30 percent of her time this next year will be spent arguing for tax changes favorable to her firm and opposing unfavorable ones.

To judge whether these activities should be encouraged by society, we find it useful to categorize the actions of individuals as productive activities and transfer activities. Each scenario represents economic activity that augments the wealth of the actors or the interests they represent. But the question of the net social impact of these activities remains. Productive activity adds not only to the personal wealth of individuals but also to the total wealth of the society. Stipes, the farmer, was transforming some inputs into output that he would consume or trade to others for their consumption. Franks, although involved in an activity that many find morally repugnant and that was illegal, was nevertheless producing. He was not only adding to his own wealth but was also engaged in providing a service for which others were willing to pay. From the viewpoint of satisfying consumer preferences, he too was adding to the total well-being of at least a segment of society.

Transfer activities add to the wealth of specific individuals or groups of individuals but reduce the wealth of other individuals or groups in the society. Because transfers consume resources, such activities decrease the total product of the society. The railroad executive, the union officer, and the corporate lawyer were engaged in attempts to secure control over existing resources at a net cost to society rather than in adding to the social product. Their gain was another's loss. Because their time and effort could have been used more productively, such activities reduced the ability of the society to produce goods and services.

Another way of viewing these activities is to measure the net change in social output. In this context, productive activity is a positive-sum game, or social interaction, that enlarges the pie. Transfer activity, on the other hand, is a negative-sum game—a series of social interactions that decreases the size of the pie. There is less after the social interaction than before.

The early American experience was one in which transfer activity was limited and productive activity encouraged. The Constitution, which reflected the thoughts not only of its framers but also of the majority of the contemporary population, severely constrained transfers. But changes in attitudes and constitutional interpretations that occurred in the latter half of the nineteenth century and the early part of the twentieth century increased the returns to engaging in transfer activity.

TWO
←——→
Analytical Framework

To analyze the likely conditions under which productive activity domi-
nates transfer activity, our approach takes the individual as the unit of
analysis. It assumes that individuals are the basis of society, that their
tastes and preferences count, and that "society" and "society's preferences" are meaningful terms only insofar as they are a shorthand for a
set of individual preferences represented by a single vector, society. The
economist James Buchanan argues that if one starts with the premise
that only individuals and their values are significant, "a criterion for
'betterness' is suggested. A situation is judged 'good' to the extent that it
allows individuals to get what they want to get, whatsoever this might be,
limited only by the principle of mutual agreement."[1] When we use the
terms positive- and negative-sum games, we refer only to the summation
of individual values. *We do not consider interpersonal utility comparisons made
by third parties.* In this book, positive-sum games for the most part refer to
transactions that expand total output. However, positive-sum games also
result from the voluntary exchange of existing output that moves output
from lower- to higher-valued alternatives. In such cases no interpersonal
utility comparison is made since the participants in the voluntary trade
judge their own preferences. It is possible to label involuntary exchanges
as positive or negative sum by making interpersonal utility comparisons,
but our analysis makes no allowance for this.

PRODUCTIVE ACTIVITY

One of the basic principles of economics, applying to both production
and exchange, is that an individual makes decisions by comparing
marginal benefits with marginal costs and that in so doing maximizes his

well-being. Input *A* will be transformed into output *X* only if the marginal cost (opportunity cost) of using *A* in this production is less than or equal to the additional value of *X* produced. Moreover, the ownership of an input or output will be exchanged for the ownership of another input or output only if the marginal value of the ownership surrendered is less than the value of ownership received.

Another principle of economics is that an individual participates in a voluntary trade with the expectation that it is a positive-sum game. In other words, no party expects to lose through a voluntary exchange of ownership rights. If one or more parties is better off and none is worse off, the transaction is positive sum from the perspective of the traders. Combining this principle with the marginal decision rule, we see that whether an individual moves resources from one use to another or trades ownership of inputs or outputs, *voluntary* activities of these types are positive-sum games for the parties voluntarily involved.

To this point, however, we have described only the end result with respect to the well-being of the parties to the activity; what is there to ensure that these trades are productive activities or positive-sum games for all of society?[2] The standard literature in economics argues that voluntary trades are positive sum for society as long as there are no externalities; that is, as long as net marginal private benefits equal net marginal social benefits, voluntary decisions are positive sum for all of society as well as for the decision makers. Alternatively, private decisions are positive sum for society when those with authority to act are accountable to society for their actions. Since those who have the authority to act determine the allocation of resources and outputs, the question is making these persons responsible for their actions. Responsibility determines who is accountable for benefits and costs, and responsibility is determined by ownership; private property institutions are therefore important because they promote productive activity.

To ensure that voluntary actions of individuals are productive, ownership must be exclusive. Property rights cannot be attenuated without incurring a social cost. For ownership to be exclusive, rights governing the use of resources must be well defined, enforced, and transferable. Definition and enforcement guarantee that all costs and benefits accrue to the actor, and transferability ensures that gains from trade can be realized. The economics literature is replete with discussions demonstrating that violation of any of these conditions generates inefficiency.[3] Whenever ownership is nonexclusive, the link between authority and responsibility is broken. When this occurs, the positive-sum actions of individuals do not necessarily result in productive activity for society. When the stream of benefits is attenuated, individuals devote too few resources to the activity; when the stream of costs is attenuated, individuals devote too many resources to the activity. This suggests that the rights structure must be an efficient one. Property rights can be well specified and enforced, but they may not allow all opportunities for productive activity to be exhausted. The definition and enforcement of an efficient set of private property rights are therefore necessary conditions for productive activity. Under these conditions an individual can enhance the productive capacity of society and at the same time increase personal wealth; that is, individuals do good while doing well.

TRANSFER ACTIVITY

Unfortunately, since property rights are not always well defined and enforced, productive activity is not the only way that an individual wealth maximizer can enhance his position. Wealth position is determined only in part by the ability of a decision maker to move inputs and outputs from lower- to higher-valued alternatives. A maximizer successful at such moves will have increased wealth. But wealth position is also determined by access to and use of resources and the outputs therefrom; in other words, by who holds the exclusive property rights. Therefore, in addition to productive activity, a decision maker can increase his wealth by devoting resources and effort to obtaining these rights.[4]

When such rights are obtained without some quid pro quo, a non-voluntary transfer takes place. The most obvious example of such transfer activity is theft. At first glance this activity might appear to be zero sum since one person's gain is another's loss. But this ignores the process through which the transfer is effected. The result of this transfer activity is *negative sum* since nothing is produced and resources are expended in the process. (The reader is reminded of our unwillingness to allow interpersonal utility comparisons.) A thief invests in physical and human capital to effect a transfer only if it nets a normal rate of return. Moreover, an owner invests in additional measures to increase the probability of capturing the return to his assets. Traditional analysis has viewed transfers of this sort as altering the distribution of income without affecting output since the total amount of goods in society remains unchanged. Thus, if A steals B's car, traditional analysis says that no social loss has occurred, assuming the value to both individuals is equal. But this ignores the consumption of resources in A's attempts to carry out the theft and B's attempts to prevent it. "The transfer itself may be costless, but the prospect of the transfer leads individuals and groups to invest resources in either attempting to obtain a transfer or to resist a transfer away from themselves. These resources represent net social waste."[5]

To reduce this waste and discourage such negative-sum games, the coercive power of government is employed to help define and enforce private rights. Police forces, courts, legislatures, and other mechanisms are used to promote exclusivity in property. Therefore, rules against transfers can be important for promoting positive-sum games. In other words, the illegalization of theft is justifiable on the grounds not only that it is immoral but also that it results in the wasteful use of resources.[6]

Using the coercive power of the state to define and enforce property rights does discourage theft, but it opens another arena for transfer activity. Clearly, any state that defines and enforces property rights can also redefine and reallocate rights. To the extent that redefinition and reallocation occur, exclusivity is reduced.[7] By altering the rules of the game, which we have defined as the specification of access to and use of resources, an individual can increase his wealth position. To the extent that redefinition and redistribution result from the legal process, transfers occur and the total productive potential of society decreases. Although this redistribution might be defended by a social welfare function, still society's maximum capacity is reduced by resources devoted to transfer activity.[8]

This raises an interesting dilemma. Allowing all transfers, including theft, to occur without regulation implies a reduction of production possibilities; but making the redistribution of private property rights illegal and enforcing the laws simply alters the arena of transfer activity. Without further information, it is not possible to determine which solution results in smaller losses.

THE CONSTITUTIONAL CONTRACT

The basic constitutional contract, however, does offer a way of reducing such resource waste. If the members of the society negotiating that

contract recognize the potential for transfer activity with its accompanying waste and make certain rules (in particular those protecting basic
rights) difficult to change, transfers are much less likely to occur. Viewed
in this manner, the constitutional contract is a fundamental set of
principles providing definition and allowing enforcement of private
rights that cannot be altered by the coercive power of government without recourse to some extraordinary process.

Such a constitutional contract must specify at least two things: the
basic rights of all individual participants in the compact and the means of
enforcing these rights. Given these specifications the state becomes
simply a protector of mutually determined rights, a "protective state."
The individual makes a trade, agreeing to surrender some freedom of
action in order to better secure his rights and to save on resources that
might otherwise go into predation and defense activities. The state in
return provides a mechanism for securing and protecting these rights.
In fulfilling this function, the state has no legal power to alter rights.
Therefore, there is no potential for legal transfers inherent in the
legitimate use of the state's coercive power.[9] The state can claim only
those resources it is granted to enable it to protect these rights. Because
of the potential free-rider problem, coercion may be necessary to collect
these resources, but any further coercion would be illegitimate.

If transfers are a major source of resource waste (that is, if they are
negative sum) and can be prevented by appropriately constructed constitutional contracts, why not solve the problem by constitutionally prohibiting all involuntary transfers? There are at least two reasons why a
society might choose not to prohibit all transfers: the "legitimacy issue"
and the "public goods problem."[10]

The legitimacy issue concerns the morality of the distribution of
rights. A society that prohibits all involuntary transfers has no mechanism
for rectifying obviously illegitimate holdings of rights. For instance, in a
nontransfer society, the United States' resolution of the slavery issue
would have been incorrect because there was a clear-cut transfer of the
rights to the income produced by a slave from the slaveholder to the
slave. If a constitutional contract is to be legitimate, the original distribution of rights under that contract must be legitimate.[11] If the original distribution was itself obtained through transfers (as in the case of slavery),
a redistribution of rights becomes necessary.

A second problem occurs because voluntary trades may not exhaust
all productive possibilities. The cost of excluding nonparticipants from

the benefits of an exchange may result in underproduction of some commodities. Consider the case of a dam that will prevent flooding and subsequent crop loss. The costs of such a dam may well be considerably less than the benefits. However, each of the farmers downstream refuses to contribute to the dam's construction because he knows that he cannot be excluded from the benefits. If the dam is built, his cropland will not be subject to flooding even though he did not pay his share of the construction costs.

Because it makes sense for members of the society to conceal their true preferences for these public goods, such goods will be underproduced in the market. Collective action, however, provides a means of raising public goods production to the optimal amount. By using the coercive power of the state to force all downstream users to contribute, dams that are public goods can be built.[12] Coercion or less than unanimous consent for decisions may be necessary in order to secure public goods that would be underproduced. The ground rules for the coercion would be specified in the constitutional contract, and agreement to be coerced would imply a perceived long-run gain for all members of the society, that is, a productive role for the state.[13]

Although a case can be made for allowing transfers for legitimacy and public goods reasons, this can generate a movement to a society dominated by transfer activity. Once the legal mechanism to deal with these two issues is established, it is difficult to control the power of government to transfer rights. "But how can government, itself the reflection of interests, establish the legitimate boundaries of self-interest, and how can it, conversely, carve out those areas of intervention that will be socially protective and collectively useful?"[14]

With regard to the legitimacy issue, if a mechanism is established by which the government can alter rights holdings because those holdings are illegitimate, what prevents any and every individual and group who desires someone else's rights from approaching the government with their particular standard of legitimacy and arguing for such a transfer? For instance, it was argued in the latter part of the nineteenth century that a railroad's right to the profits from transporting farmers' commodities should be limited. The attempt to resolve this dilemma resulted in numerous situations similar to those depicted in chapter 1. Once this issue was carried to government, many resources were devoted to resolving it. In this particular case, the railroads not only gained the right to their profits but also were able to limit competition.[15] Similarly, to use one of the scenarios from chapter 1, much transfer activity has occurred because of attempts to resolve legitimacy issues through taxation. Once taxes were conceived as a means of removing unwarranted (illegitimate?) earnings from certain individuals in the society, the tax laws became fair game for anyone interested in gaining wealth through nonproductive means. The current lack of general agreement on the legitimacy of much economic activity (for example, oil company profits) is a source of transfer activity.

The same difficulty exists with the use of the coercive power of the state to resolve the public goods problem. Nonvoluntary transfers for the purpose of providing public goods may become positive-sum transactions. The problem is one of accurately defining a public good. If this cannot be specified and therefore limited to only those goods from which nonpaying consumers cannot be excluded, legitimate powers specified in the constitution can and will be used for other types of transfer activity. Negative-sum games will result. Transfer mechanisms dealing with illegitimacy and public goods allow the camel's nose under the tent. The problem is keeping the beast from obtaining full entry.

THE MIX OF PRODUCTIVE AND TRANSFER ACTIVITY

The legitimacy issue and the public goods problem suggest reasons for the existence of transfer activity within a constitutional contract, but they do not explain the fluctuations in the mix of productive and transfer activity. A complete explanation of changes in this mix has yet to evolve, but the standard economics analysis suggests at least two variables. First, on the demand side, the growth process resulting from productive activity provides an incentive to seek transfers. Second, on the supply side, the constraints on transfer activity in the constitutional contract are subject to change in accord with contemporary ideology.

The demand for transfer activity exists because it offers a potential method of increasing personal wealth, but this demand is stimulated by productive activity and the accompanying growth process. A constitutional contract that provides only minimal protective and productive roles for the state (that is, equates private and social rates of return) will result in a dynamic economy where resources are continually re-evaluated and moved to higher-valued uses. Positive-sum, productive activity will increase the aggregate wealth of the society. The demand side of the market will change because of higher incomes and shifting tastes, and the supply side will adjust to new technology and improved efficiency. In addition to increasing aggregate wealth, this dynamic process will alter the wealth position of individuals holding legitimate rights. The economist Douglass North describes the dynamics as follows:

> In effect, an ownership structure that provided incentives for efficient re-source allocation (i.e., a set of property rights that made the private rate of return on innovation, investment in human capital, etc., approach the social rate) would be essential. But we should note immediately that the conse-quences must be destabilizing, since technological change, the spread of more efficient markets, etc., would alter relative prices and the opportunity cost of constituents and lead eventually to conflicts with the fundamental ownership structure of property rights.[16]

The *absolute* wealth position of some members of society may decline as demand for their goods or services declines; the *relative* wealth position of others may decline as demand for the goods and services of other rights holders rises. In either case, there will be an incentive to recover a loss through transfer activity. This suggests that a productive society will gen-erate its own destabilizing forces by increasing the demand for transfer activity.

Whether these increased demands are met, of course, depends on the nature of the constitutional contract. Where there is no question over the nature of rights and the legitimacy of title, little transfer activity will evolve whatever the demand. The freedom of speech and freedom of press amendments in the Bill of Rights are examples of relatively unambiguous rights. Although these amendments have been subject to interpretation, they have not allowed extensive amounts of transfer activity.

Where the constitutional contract is more ambiguous, however, the amount of transfer activity depends on interpretation, which in turn depends on ideology. In other words, the amount of transfer activity relative to productive activity is a function of social attitudes regarding the sanctity of individual rights as reflected through the court system. Ideas do matter. As long as rights are considered inviolable, transfers are much less likely to be effected through the coercive power of govern-ment. But if all rights are thought to be held at the mercy of the state, transfer activity is much more likely to prevail. Unfortunately, we do not have a theory that explains how and why ideas change, but we do know that change occurs. These changes, we argue, are a part of the exogenous forces that have given birth to the transfer society.

Theoretical analysis has taken us a long way toward understanding the nature of the constitutional contract; but, as James Buchanan suggests, "once it is recognized that observed institutions of legal-political order exist only in a historical setting, the attraction of trying to analyze conceptual origins independently of historical process is severely weakened."[17] American history provides an interesting opportunity to apply the productive/transfer activity paradigm since the American political experiment has been one that consciously attempted to encourage productive activity and discourage transfer activity through a carefully reasoned, written constitution. In our view, the potential for transfers was very low in the first part of the nineteenth century, but changes in the basic rules of the game have led to social waste through the transfer process. Consequently our society is presently operating far below its full productive potential. We live in a transfer society.

THREE

←——→

Our Institutional Inheritance

A major difficulty with writing any history is that it necessitates stepping into a sequence of events at a point in time and therefore disrupts whatever flow there might be. Nonetheless, we must start and have chosen as our starting point the formal birth of the new nation with the writing of the Declaration of Independence. To reduce the disruption of this starting point, however, it is important to understand the historical setting within which this birth occurred.

Having celebrated the nation's bicentennial, most of us are aware of the importance of the past 200 years, but we should also recognize that the colonial period was nearly as long. With the settlement of Jamestown in 1607, immigrants began the arduous task of establishing permanent residences on the East Coast. The records of the initial years are filled with horror stories of starvation and suffering as the colonists searched for products and crops that would sustain a viable economic community. From the Chesapeake Bay region to the northern reaches of New England, the colonists found products ranging from tobacco to ships with profitable markets throughout the Old World. The success of their efforts is evidenced by recent findings suggesting that economic growth during the first century of inhabitance may have been as high as it has been since 1840.[1] Hence from early in the seventeenth century there was little doubt that the economic importance of the New World settlements would continue and perhaps even increase.

But the search for economic viability was but a small part of the adjustment process faced by the colonists. Many economic and social forces led to changes in the institutional framework.

PRIVATE PROPERTY IN THE ENGLISH TRADITION

According to Douglass North, "the institutions that the English set-tler brought with him provided a hospitable background for growth."[2] To the economic historian, such an assertion is unsurprising since ex-pansion of the British empire to North America came on the eve of the Industrial Revolution. But behind North's statement is more than the rise of industrialization, for, as he and Robert Thomas have shown in *The Rise of the Western World*,[3] the foundation necessary for England to achieve sustained economic growth had evolved over several centuries.

In 1066 at the time of the Norman Conquest, economic conditions in Western Europe and more specifically England were considerably differ-ent from what they were six centuries later. Perhaps the most important was the lower population density. Relatively vast areas of wilderness existed, with settlement concentrated on the production unit of the day, the manor. On these nearly self-sufficient "farms," scarce labor was com-bined with abundant land to produce food, clothing, and what few manufactured goods there were. The scarcity of labor and the abundance of land have led many to ask why production took place on manors rather than on individual farms. Why did the laborers, or serfs, allow themselves to be tied to a system that required them to provide numerous services to the lord of the manor? Was this not enslavement? One answer to this ques-tion relies on a contractual model or theory of the state similar to that pre-sented in chapter 2. In this framework feudalism and manorialism were not slave systems but arrangements that provided protection and justice, both integral parts of the productive process, in the most efficient manner. Lords provided enforcement of the rules of the game in return for services and dues from the serfs. The definition of these rules came from the manorial courts, which determined the "customs of the manor." Granted, the terms of the contract did not always favor the serfs, who often fled to cities to avoid the system; however, the relative bargaining power of the contractual parties, lord and serf, did fluctuate over time. As population and military technology changed, the terms of the contract changed.[4] The former altered the relation between the laborer and the "state," and the latter altered the relation among various states. The precise model that specifies the interaction of these variables and the rules of the game has been and will continue to be debated by scholars, but this debate is not our concern here. The importance of this for colonial institu-tional inheritance is that in the transition from manorialism to the nation-state, a contract specifying certain rights evolved between the individual and the state.

The customs of the manor were one part of this contract. On a manor a serf was granted the right to till certain strips of land or to graze a specified number of cattle in the common pasture and in return was required to pay both labor and dues in kind to the lord. "His condition, however, was mitigated by the growth of the custom of the manor, which at any rate fixed the exactions he laboured under and secured him in his hereditary holding. Like the freeman he attended the manorial court, which declared the custom of the manor and its working."[5] "Thus the customs of the manor became the unwritten 'constitution,' or the fundamental institutional arrangement of an essentially anarchic world."[6]

The second important part of the constitutional contract is found in the Magna Carta of 1215. Although originally a charter assuring the privileges of the aristocracy, it did formally establish the principle of limitation of government (in this case the king) through fundamental law. Subsequent interpretations, however, have broadened its application to include protection of the rights of all Englishmen, not just the select few included in the original charter.[7]

Although the general framework of fundamental law was established with the Magna Carta, further development was necessary before the English constitution reached its full fruition. There was considerable controversy in the fifteenth and sixteenth centuries about the relative roles of king and Parliament, but the significant institutional innovations came in the seventeenth century. One individual of major influence was Sir Edward Coke, who served for a time as chief justice of the king's bench. To him common law, the accumulated legal traditions of the society, served as a very real check on the power of the king. Coke argued that common law should also serve as a check on parliamentary action.[8] Thus the rise in the importance of common law gave additional credence to the concept that government was to operate only within certain specified boundaries.

The seventeenth century was characterized by considerable political turmoil, consisting mainly of conflict between king and Parliament over their respective rights. It has been argued elsewhere that this period of conflict introduced enough uncertainty into government that transfer activity was discouraged; that is, special interest groups in the society were not sure who had the power to confer and maintain privileges, and thus it did not pay them to attempt to get special favors from either king or Parliament.[9] The conflict culminated in the Glorious Revolution of 1688, which clearly established dual centers of power in England, with both the king and Parliament having certain rights, but with both subject to the constraints of common law.[10]

Hence by the time of significant settlement in the American colonies, there was an English constitution, which, although unwritten and in some cases ambiguous, did specify some rights of individuals and government. Despite some mercantilist elements in the economy, the institutional structure encouraged productive activity or positive-sum games more than that of earlier periods. During the seventeenth century, patent laws that encouraged innovation were established, many feudal tenures were abolished, joint stock companies were encouraged, and labor and capital mobility were increased by eliminating industrial regulation, guilds, and monopoly patents.

> England, after an inauspicious start, by 1700 was experiencing sustained economic growth. It had developed an efficient set of property rights embedded in the common law. Besides the removal of hindrances to the allocation of resources both in the factor and product markets, England had begun to protect private property in knowledge with its patent law. The stage was now set for the industrial revolution.[11]

Of course the efficient set of property rights to which North and Thomas refer here must be understood in a historical context. They were efficient relative to England's history and relative to most of Europe. There were elements of transfer activity, but the colonists did inherit a set of institutions that provided a reasonably hospitable background for growth.

POLITICAL THOUGHT ON LIBERTY

The change in the political framework as Western Europe moved from feudal society to the nation-state caused an enormous amount of discussion and writing by leading thinkers of the period. Indeed, four of the major shapers of modern political thought were concentrated in a relatively short period: Thomas Hobbes, 1588–1679; John Locke, 1632–1704; Jean Jacques Rousseau, 1712–1778; and Edmund Burke, 1729–1797. For these men and many lesser-known individuals, numerous questions were created by the move from a civil government that was quite clearly expected to be under theocratic control to a nation-state that claimed there were no limits on its power. First, they wrestled with the question of the nature of the state. What justifies it? What, if anything, limits it? Although the debate over these issues greatly influenced the American colonists, we touch only lightly on the principal ideas that shaped their conception of government.

Two major themes impacted American institutions: natural rights and the compact theory of the state. From these followed two secondary concepts—popular sovereignty and the right of revolution. Since Locke was the leading proponent of these themes and a political theorist who had significant influence on colonial thought, we concentrate on his theory.[12] Locke's major contribution was that the individual rather than the state was the locus of power, or rights. Although previous thinkers had discussed the idea of a "natural order," or a concept of justice that was independent of society's actions, Locke made it quite clear that society does not create rights, that an individual possesses them even in the absence of organized society, and that, as the proprietor of his own person and property, the individual owes nothing to society for these rights. In Locke's words:

> To understand Political Power right, and derive it from its Original, we must consider what State all Men are naturally in, and that is, a *State of perfect Freedom* to order their Actions, and dispose of their Possessions, and Persons as they think fit, within the bounds of the Law of Nature, without asking leave, or depending upon the Will of any other Man.[13]

Furthermore, since the individual has a natural right to his own body and his own labor, he also has a natural right to other property with which he mixes his labor; that is, individual property rights follow from natural rights.

The belief that the individual was the locus of all rights led Locke to conclude that individuals could contract with others to form a civil society. This society, established for the sole purpose of securing existing rights, is created by and dependent on the will of the individual members and has no separate power or rights of its own. It does have the power to enforce rights, but this power exists only as long as the members will its continuance.

From this set of precepts, it follows that if the social compact is violated (that is, if the state exceeds the powers delegated to it by the members of the society), its members have the right and indeed the duty to revolt. For Locke, revolution was an appropriate precondition to the re-establishment of another social compact, again based upon popular sovereignty.

Although Locke's work was not particularly useful and, in some cases, even contradictory as a specific blueprint for operating a government,[14] his and other basic philosophical concepts about rights and the state were read, accepted, and implemented by the colonists. In fact, the Declaration of Independence is an excellent summary of the Lockean position, stating very succinctly the doctrine of natural rights, the duty of government to protect these rights, the idea of popular sovereignty, and a long list of the violations of the social compact that justified revolution.

REVOLUTIONARY CHANGE

By the beginning of the eighteenth century, the "essential conditions had been created for bringing the private rate of return close enough to the social rate, so that productivity increase was built into the system in Holland and England (*as well as in the New World*). Over the next century these conditions in these areas induced a revolution in technology which gradually spread over much of the rest of Europe and *satellite colonies* overseas as well [emphasis added]."[15] If the colonies did indeed inherit an efficient institutional structure conducive to growth and growth was in fact the outcome, why then did the colonists choose to change this structure through violent revolution?

The causes of the American Revolution are not our central concern, but the concept of governmental transfers may offer an explanation. The general impression that one receives from comparisons of the benefits and costs of colonial membership in the British empire is that the *average* burden of this membership was not large.[16] But the burden came in the form of taxes placed on enumerated products, which translated into transfers of income from specific groups to other groups through the coercive power of Parliament. Although the average burden may have been small, individual burdens may have been quite significant. If those who directly bore the burden (the merchants) were politically influential, one would expect significant and effective protests to occur. Moreover, there can be little doubt that the colonists were alarmed by the ability of Crown and Parliament to transfer rights away from them without regard for constitutional rules. The colonists saw such legislation as the Stamp Act, the Tea Act, the Intolerable Acts, and the Navigation Acts as efforts by the Crown to limit liberty and attenuate private property rights. Although for each individual or group a different set of rights was at stake, to an extent they shared a common vision of the future. With increasing dismay, the colonists

> saw in the measures taken by the British government and in the actions of officials in the colonies something for which their peculiar inheritance of thought had prepared them only too well, something they had long conceived to be a possibility in view of the known tendencies of history and of the present state of affairs in England. They saw about them, with increasing clarity, not merely mistaken, or even evil, policies violating the principles upon which freedom rested, but what appeared to be evidence of nothing less than a deliberate assault launched surreptitiously by plotters against liberty both in England and in America.[17]

The Stamp Act, for example, was more than "an impolitic and unjust law that threatened the priceless right of the individual to retain possession of his property until he or his chosen representative voluntarily gave it up to another";[18] it was part of a general trend by the English government to ignore the constitutional rights of colonists.

The institutional inheritance described above suggests that the colonists believed that their freedom and liberty derived from the constitutional restraints on government. From the time of William the Conqueror, the English had experienced a slow institutional evolution to the point that, in the eighteenth century, freedom and private rights to property were afforded some protection from arbitrary seizure, a necessary precondition for the Industrial Revolution and the accompanying economic growth. Moreover, it was a concern of the philosphers of the day. Locke understood that sacrificing natural rights to a government that knew no restraints would lead to slavery rather than freedom. And Adam Smith, whose writings influenced colonial thought,[19] also recognized that freedom and growth could come only if government's ability to weaken individual rights was constrained. Out of the eighteenth-century libertarian philosophies two themes ring clear:

> The first is the belief that power is evil, a necessity perhaps but an evil necessity; that it is infinitely corrupting; and that it must be controlled, limited, restricted in every way compatible with a minimum of civil order . . . [And the second] the belief that through the ages it had been

privilege—artificial, man-made and man-secured privilege, ascribed to some and denied to others mainly at birth—that, more than anything else except the misuse of power, had crushed men's hopes for fulfillment.[20]

To individuals involved in the Revolution, it was the use of this power and privilege that usurped private rights guaranteed in the unwritten constitutional contract.

While the English saw their actions as necessary to finance colonial defense (a protective function of the state), the colonists viewed them as more than an attempt to impose arbitrary power, "a deliberate design to destroy the constitutional safeguards of liberty, which only concerted resistance—violent resistance if necessary—could effectively oppose."[21] The actions of Parliament before the Declaration of Independence made its intention all the more clear. The Navigation Acts, the Stamp Act, and the Townshend Acts (notably the Tea Act) were all examples of governmental efforts that burdened the colonists and usurped private rights. But these by no means exhausted the list. The Boston Port Act restricting trade into and out of the largest colonial port, the Massachusetts Government Act stripping citizens of constitutional rights by granting full power to the executive, the Quartering Act extending the power of the military to utilize civilian housing, and the Administration of Justice Act permitting trials to be transferred to the mother country were all implemented following the Boston Tea Party. Such acts contributed to the colonists' growing belief that the English government's ability to transfer rights was unlimited.

The impact of the violations of constitutional rights effected through these acts differed, but the weight of the burden finally tipped the balance in favor of revolution. The final result was a document that made clear the general principles uniting the colonists—principles that they believed were embedded in the British constitution.

As they themselves keenly realized, their interpretation of the English constitution was the point on which their understanding of the Revolution hinged. For it was the principles of the English constitution that the colonists clung to throughout the dozen years of controversy with the mother country. They said over and over again that it was "both the letter and the spirit of the British constitution" which justified their resistance. Even as late as 1776 they assured themselves there was "no room at all to doubt, but we have justice and the British constitution on our side." This repeated insistence that they were the true guardians of the British constitution, even enjoying it "in greater purity and perfection" than

Englishmen themselves, lent a curious conservative color to the American Revolution.[22]

The Declaration of Independence attempted to make this point clear by declaring that men are created with certain inalienable rights, among which are life, liberty, the pursuit of happiness, *and* the right to establish a government that would ensure these rights. Under the social contract with England these rights had been violated, making revolution appropriate. Given the weakening of what were thought to be sanctified rights held by individuals in the colonies, it was necessary to declare the existence of such rights and then to resanctify them. Declaring their existence was one thing, but ensuring that they would not be attenuated was quite another. The Declaration of Independence accomplished the first task by stating the purpose of government; it was left to the Constitution, however, to provide the operational structure for that purpose.

The colonists did in fact inherit much of their institutional framework although they had to engage in armed resistance to retain that inheritance. This resistance was a form of institutional change or, in this case perhaps more appropriately, institutional re-establishment. The "revolution of sober expectations," as Martin Diamond has called it,[23] was a conservative revolution that attempted to reinstate what the colonists thought was the status quo ante. Even some Englishmen viewed the events preceding the Revolution as violations of the constitutional contract that would eventually snuff out liberty and saw America as a last hope. This same thought was expressed by colonist Thomas Paine in 1776:

> Every spot of the Old World is overrun with oppression. Freedom hath been hunted round the globe. Asia and Africa have long expelled her. Europe regards her like a stranger, and England hath given her warning to depart. O! receive the fugitive, and prepare in time an asylum for mankind.[24]

FOUR

⟵⟶

The Constitutional Contract

> To perceive the true purposes of the American Revolution, it is
> wise to ignore some of the more grandiloquent declamations of
> the moment . . . and to look at the kinds of political activity the
> Revolution unleashed. This activity took the form of constitu-
> tion-making, above all.
>
> *Irving Kristol*
> *"The American Revolution as a Successful Revolution"*

Despite the strong background in private rights, the character of the
colonial economy was not completely laissez-faire. In fact, J. R. T.
Hughes argues that social control pervaded the colonial economy.[1] The
lack of a well-specified English constitution and the impact of the
doctrine of mercantilism meant that the government made many economic decisions. Colonial America was a mixture of both market and
nonmarket controls, with nonmarket restraints dominating some aspects
of life. Transfers were prevalent, on the part of both the English
Parliament and local jurisdictions. The revolutionaries' visions of the
society that they hoped would result from independence included
security of rights from that necessary evil, government. Being "conceived in liberty" was the result of our institutional inheritance, but
transforming this conception into a working society required more than
a revolution. The colonists engaged in the revolution of sober expectations had to focus their energies on the ambitious task of formulating a
new set of rules.

POST-REVOLUTIONARY POLITICAL PHILOSOPHY

In sharp contrast to current ideology, the legacy of 1776 held fast to
three basic political principles that greatly influenced the nature of the

U.S. Constitution. First, freedom and liberty were the fundamental goals of society, and it was to this end that all organizational efforts should be directed. Second, because of man's selfish nature, general goodwill was insufficient to achieve liberty. And third, government was necessary to reconcile the first two, but government itself was imperfect and therefore a necessary evil to be constrained appropriately.[2] Support for all three of these beliefs is found in the thoughts and writings of the revolutionaries.

Such famous cries as Patrick Henry's "Give me liberty or give me death" illustrate the importance that the colonists placed on freedom from arbitrary governmental action, but they sought more freedoms than those eventually listed in the Bill of Rights. In the words of colonist James Sullivan, "every member of civil society has a clear right to gain all the property which vigilance and industry, regulated by the laws of the state, can bestow upon him."[3] In other words, a major component of liberty was that property rights belonged to individuals and were not to be altered by government. Natural rights existed, and the right to property was an important part of them. E. A. J. Johnson's succinct paraphrase of the agrarian liberal George Logan illustrates contemporary thinking on property rights: "Every property owner . . . ought to have complete freedom to do whatever he wished with his property. Civil law should enforce contracts but ought never attempt to restrict entrepreneurial freedom. Competition and free trade will result in just prices for all commmodities and ensure the best rewards for human endeavor."[4] The free and unrestrained alienation of property, not the redistribution of property rights among the citizens, was to provide equal opportunity. The leaders of the American Revolution "understood what their contemporary, Adam Smith, understood and what we today have some difficulty in understanding: namely, that poverty is abolished by economic growth, not by economic redistribution—there is never enough to distribute—and that rebellions, by creating instability and uncertainty, have mischievous consequences for economic growth."[5]

A strong belief in private property meant neither that the Founding Fathers were anarchists nor that they believed that unconstrained self-interest always produced social good. Rather they believed that some rights had to be ceded to the state in order that the remaining rights could be secure. This Lockean view of government was well expressed by Noah Webster: "Each individual pursues his own interest; and consults the good of others no farther than his own interest requires. Hence, the necessity of laws which respect the whole body collectively, and restrain the pursuits of individuals when they infringe the public rights."[6]

The colonists recognized that self-imposed morality might on occasion be sufficient to restrain selfish behavior, but they also held that "it is unalterable law, that man shall be guided by self-interest."[7] This did not mean that self-interest would automatically reduce social output, but that it could do so if not constrained and guided by an appropriate set of rules.

A contract that ensured freedom and secured property rights for all in the context of this view of human nature was to be the basis for social organization. Some form of government was deemed necessary to perform protective and productive activities, but the colonists believed that such a government could favor special interests at the expense of the public good. It was not then and is not today difficult to find agreement that private dealings among individuals are guided by self-interest; but it is today sometimes implied that dealings in the public sector are guided by public interest. The Founding Fathers lived under no such illusion. To John Taylor the formation of pressure groups was for one purpose alone: "a transfer of private or public property, or both, from individuals or nations, to orders, corporations or to other individuals."[8] The likelihood that individuals could transcend their own special interests was small. "Hence, all legislation will be tinctured with partiality for one interest or another because public policy is formulated not by objective and disinterested lawgivers, but by legislators confronted by the 'importunity of partial interests,' by men who themselves represent particular interests."[9] In the *Social Philosophy of John Taylor*, Eugene T. Mudge discusses the issue in terms of two societies, one that operates on the basis of individuals entering mutual agreements producing positive-sum results and one that "lives, parasitically, by law and privilege. Government is created to favor the first interest, but it is often corrupted by the latter."[10] To protect and produce, government had to be given legitimate coercive power. To ensure that this power was not corrupted and individual rights were not violated was a central concern of the political theorists and practitioners of the latter part of the eighteenth century.

THE FEDERALIST PAPERS

Although the *Federalist Papers* were written after the Constitution in order to secure its ratification, these essays constitute the best existing

summary of the political ideology of that document. The authors of the
Federalist Papers realized that great care was required if the new government they were constructing was to have enough power to carry out its
responsibilities but not so much power that the rights of individuals
would be infringed.

> Among the difficulties encountered by the convention, a very important
> one must have lain in combining the requisite stability and energy in
> government with the inviolable attention due to liberty and to the republi-
> can form.[11]

> In framing a government which is to be administered by men over men,
> the great difficulty lies in this: you must first enable the government to
> control the governed; and in the next place oblige it to control itself.[12]

To secure such control over government one cannot rely simply on
electing the "right" people.

> It is in vain to say that enlightened statesmen will be able to adjust these
> clashing interests and render them all subservient to the public good.
> Enlightened statesmen will not always be at the helm . . . We well know that
> neither moral nor religious motives can be relied on as an adequate
> control.[13]

This reluctance to entrust the innate goodness of man with the responsibility of limiting government resulted from the authors' view of man's
basic nature. To rely solely on goodness

> would be to forget that men are ambitious, vindictive, and rapacious . . .
> Has it not, on the contrary, invariably been found that momentary
> passions, and immediate interests, have a more active and imperious
> control over human conduct than general or remote considerations of
> policy, utility, or justice?[14]

Because of this view, the framers of the Constitution had carefully
constructed the appropriate institutional arrangements to channel man's
self-interest.

> Ambition must be made to counteract ambition. The interest of the man
> must be connected with the constitutional rights of the place. It may be a
> reflection on human nature that such devices should be necessary to control
> the abuses of government. But what is government itself but the greatest of
> all reflections on human nature? If men were angels, no government would
> be necessary. If angels were to govern men, neither external nor internal
> controls on government would be necessary.[15]

The main institutional innovation that resulted from these concepts was a document that laid out clearly what government could and could not do and specified certain rights that were not alterable by ordinary governm ental action.

> The important distinction so well understood in America between a Constitution established by the people and unalterable by the government, and a law established by the government and alterable by the government, seems to have been little understood and less observed in any other country.[16]

> There is no position which depends on clearer principles than that every act of a delegated authority, contrary to the tenor of the commission under which it is exercised, is void. No legislative act, therefore, contrary to the Constitution, can be valid ... A constitution is, in fact, and must be regarded by the judges as, a fundamental law ... They ought to regulate their decisions by the fundamental laws rather than by those which are not fundamental.[17]

The Founding Fathers saw clearly the potential of democratic government to take actions that were not consonant with the original social contract. It is true that "the people are the only legitimate fountain of power,"[18] but that does not mean that decisions based on simple majority vote are always legitimate. Some additional protection of individual rights is in order.

> When a majority is included in a faction, the form of popular government, on the other hand, enables it to sacrifice to its ruling passion or interest both the public good and the rights of other citizens. To secure the public good and private rights against the danger of such a faction, and at the same time to preserve the spirit and the form of popular government, is then the great object to which our inquiries are directed.[19]

Thus the framers of the Constitution had attempted to design a government with checks and balances and clear limitations that would not result in a "tyranny of the majority." The stability of rights was important not only as a first principle of legitimate government but also as a necessary condition for economic growth.

> The diversity in the faculties of men, from which the rights of property originate, is not less an insuperable obstacle to a uniformity of interests. The protection of these faculties is the first object of government.[20]

> In another point of view, great injury results from an unstable government. The want of confidence in the public councils damps every useful

undertaking, the success and profit of which may depend on a continuance of existing arrangements. What prudent merchant will hazard his fortunes in any new branch of commerce when he knows not but that his plans may be rendered unlawful before they can be executed? What farmer or manufacturer will lay himself out for the encouragement given to any particular cultivation or establishment, when he can have no assurance that his preparatory labors and advances will not render him a victim to an inconstant government?[21]

Although the Constitution was a controversial document, the real debate during this period was not about the principles outlined here. After the experience with Britain, even the Anti-Federalists were strongly committed to the concept that government should be limited. They also "expected power to be abused" and considered it "the duty of those framing a government, which might control the destiny of future generations, to guard against even the bare possibility of future tyranny."[22] The main issue for those who opposed the Constitution was the adequacy of the proposed limits on government, particularly at the federal level. The point we wish to emphasize is that most political spokesmen of the time agreed on the necessity of creating an institution that constrained man's selfish desires, both within and without government. Governmental coercion always carries the potential for negative-sum games; therefore such constraints were seen as essential in creating the potential for a productive (positive-sum game) society.

THE CONSTITUTION AND TRANSFERS

From this political-economic ideology emerged the rules governing social interaction. Since the Declaration of Independence only proclaimed the right to institute a new government but did not specifiy its operations, the rebellious colonists were in a position to establish whatever framework they believed would achieve their common goals. Individual state constitutions began to emerge as soon as the Continental Congress ordered the formal abolition of royal authority in the states in May 1776. Some of these constitutions differed radically from the colonial charters, while others merely recodified existing rules. In most cases the distinction between constitution and general statute law was not recognized. Between 1776 and 1777 none of the state conventions submitted their constitutions to the people for approval. Massachusetts was the first state, in 1777, to apply Locke's theory of social contract by submitting a legislature-drafted constitution for ratification, to the populace, who rejected it on the grounds that it was not the product of an independent convention. A new state constitution did not come until 1780 when a two-thirds majority of the voters ratified a compact from such a convention.

Although not all constitutions were as democratic as this, the political economy of the Revolution did set the stage for the concept of constitutional supremacy. And with this concept came that of judicial review. In *Federalist 10*, Madison recognized that legislatures could not be relied on to judge their own actions.

> No man is allowed to be a judge in his own cause, because his interest would certainly bias his judgment, and, not improbably, corrupt his integrity. With equal, nay with greater reason, a body of men are unfit to be both judges and parties at the same time; yet what are many of the most important acts of legislation but so many judicial determinations, not indeed concerning the rights of single persons, but concerning the rights of large bodies of citizens?[23]

The establishment of government necessitated the surrender of some natural rights to the legislature; the constitution was to ensure that retained rights were not usurped by government. As early as 1786 in the Rhode Island case of *Trevett* v. *Weeden*, James Varnum, attorney for the defense, argued that it was the responsibility of the judiciary to gauge all legislative acts against the constitution and "reject all acts of the legislature that are contrary to the trust reposed in them by the people."[24] The British government's unwillingness to respect the rights that the colonists believed they possessed had provoked the American Revolution, and the independent colonists responded at the state level by sanctifying these rights in written social compacts.

But the real difficulties and controversies concerning the rules of government were not at the state level; rather the major concern was protecting individual liberties from national meddling. The initial effort to solve this issue came in the form of the Articles of Confederation, which were ratified by all states by 1781. The Articles' limitations on transfer activity were more extensive than those in the Constitution. Since the Articles denied Congress the powers of taxation and regulation of commerce, they restricted the amount of resources the national government could control. The ratification of the Articles marked a

significant victory for the states' rights group, who secured a clause
providing for the "sovereignty, freedom and independence" of the
separate states. Since the cost of voting with the feet was lower at the state
level than at the national level, competition among sovereign states
helped ensure basic liberties.

On the other hand, the Articles of Confederation gave so little power
to the national government that it was unable to undertake the protective
and productive functions demanded at that level. For revenue the central
government had to rely on state governments to collect levies imposed by
Congress, but the states were so derelict in their duties that the
Confederation government was plunged into bankruptcy. In the absence
of effective coercive power, free riding can dominate. And free riding
was exactly what many of the states chose to do.

The ability of the individual states to impose internal trade barriers
diluted many of the economic benefits of union. Economies of scale and
specialization were hampered, and state laws requiring use of the state's
own currency or penalizing out-of-state currency raised transaction
costs.

Another problem was that state courts were called on to enforce
national laws since there was no federal judiciary. Again, however, the
states were delinquent in their responsibilities. "They flouted the Treaty
of Peace of 1783 with England: their legislatures violated its provisions
at will, while their courts generally refused to recognize any rights other
than those arising under the laws of their own respective states."[25]
Compounding the problems of enforcing federal laws were problems of
lawlessness in the states. Shays's Rebellion in Massachusetts in 1786 is
perhaps most famous incident where disrespect for private property
rights and obligation of contract signaled that changes in the rules were
necessary if transfer activity was not to dominate. Daniel Shays led an
armed insurrection in an effort to forestall bankruptcy proceedings
against economically beleaguered farmers and to secure legislation that
would allow these farmers release from their contracts. This threat to
private property rights greatly alarmed many of the colonists. To James
Madison, the need for reform was self-evident.

> The sober people of America are weary of the fluctuating policy which has
> directed the public councils. They have seen with regret and indignation
> that sudden changes and legislative interferences, in cases affecting per-
> sonal rights, become jobs in the hands of enterprising and influential
> speculators, and snares to the more industrious and less informed part of

the community. They have seen, too, that one legislative interference is but
the first link of a long chain of repetitions, every subsequent interference
being naturally produced by the effects of the preceding. They very rightly
infer, therefore, that some thorough reform is wanting, which will banish
speculations on public measures, inspire a general prudence and industry,
and give a regular course to the business of society.[26]

The reform to which Madison referred was, of course, the Constitution, and it was this document that outlined the protective and productive
roles of the federal government and specified the retained rights of
individuals. Drafting the Constitution was no small task in a country
with such diverse interests. In addition to the interests of those who fa-
vored the Articles of Confederation (chiefly from the smaller states) and
the Federalists (mostly from the larger states), there were the interests of
agriculture, manufacturing, and commerce. Despite these interests,
however, one theme united the framers of the Constitution: the provision of liberty and security of individual rights. The basic issue was "you
must first enable the government to control the governed; and in the
next place oblige it to control itself."[27] Views on accomplishing this varied
among the interest groups, and it took some bargaining and maneuver-
ing to reach agreement on a document suitable for presentation to the
people for ratification. Issues involving the operation of the government
through the executive and legislative branches were important but
minor in comparison to the issue of supremacy of the Constitution and
the federal laws passed under that document.

One basic difference between the Articles of Confederation and the
Constitution was the relation between the federal government and the
states and citizens. States' rights groups remained steadfast to the
concept of state sovereignty, while the Federalists argued that this
conception had produced chaos under the Articles. But nearly all agreed
that the role and scope of the national government should be limited. In
the end the Federalists won. The federal government was granted the
power of coercion to achieve its specified goals, and this coercion did not
depend on the state governments for execution. The states' sovereignty,
however, was not entirely clear since the Constitution did not specify
who, the national or the state government, was to interpret the document. It finally took the Civil War to lay to rest any doubts about the
supremacy of the federal union.

The second basic difference between the Articles and the Constitution
was the establishment of a federal judiciary, which eventually assumed

the role of interpreting the Constitution. The Constitution did not provide specifically for appeals from state to federal courts, nor did it empower the Supreme Court to interpret the compact and determine the limits of national and state authority under it. Although vagueness on this issue led to debates (which have continued until today), the compact clearly allowed for the possibility of appeals, and following the Judiciary Act of 1789, the Supreme Court assumed the final power to rule on the constitutionality of both state and federal actions.[28]

Once the draft document was signed on September 17, 1787, by 39 members of the constitutional convention, the next task was to obtain ratification. During the ensuing year the battle between the Federalists and the Anti-Federalists raged, but by June 1788 the required number of states had ratified the Constitution. Concern over the absence of a bill of rights and fear that state sovereignty would be destroyed were countered by the Federalist arguments discussed above. The fundamental rules supported by the Federalists "gave recognition to several ideas of colonial and Revolutionary political philosophy: the compact theory of the state, the notion of a written constitution, the conception of constitutional supremacy and limited legislative capacity, the doctrine of natural rights, and the separation of powers."[29] America's experiment with limited government had begun. The Constitution became the supreme law of the land and controlled both state and federal governmental actions. Although the national government was given the power to tax and regulate interstate commerce, it was generally conceived that these powers would be used for only limited purposes, the most important of which was the provision of peace and law and order.

In addition to the general theme of limited government and security of private rights for the citizens of the United States, the Constitution and the Bill of Rights contained some specific guarantees against arbitrary governmental violation of rights. When we think of specific rights guaranteed by the Constitution, the first ten amendments—freedom of speech, press, religion—immediately come to mind. To be sure, these are important elements of liberty and must be guarded from the transfer process. For the remainder of this book, however, we concentrate on three other provisions of our social contract that are important to the transfer process as it relates to economic activities: (1) Article I, Section 10, the contract clause of the Constitution, which provides that "no state shall . . . pass any Bill of Attainder, ex post facto law or law impairing the Obligation of Contracts"; (2) Article I,

Section 8, the commerce clause of the Constitution, which gives Congress the power "to regulate Commerce with foreign nations, and among the several States, and with the Indian Tribes"; and (3) the Fifth Amendment (and later the Fourteenth), which provides that no person shall "be deprived of life, liberty or property, without due process of law." Throughout the history of the United States all three have significantly affected the security of private property rights. Before specifically discussing the interpretation of these provisions over time, let us consider the general implications of each for the transfer process.

If social output is to be maximized through an autonomous market system of individuals making free choices concerning privately owned resources, individuals must be able to enter into agreements that result in positive-sum games. It is clear that if the state is allowed to impair the obligations of contracts freely entered into by individuals or groups, the likelihood of positive-sum exchanges is diminished. In all agreements there is some probability of default by one of the parties, but allowing governmental intervention into the contractual process increases the degree of uncertainty. "The constitutional status quo offers the basis upon which individuals may form expectations about the course of events, expectations which are necessary for rational planning."[30] The Federalists recognized the importance of this stability. "Laws in violation of private contracts, as they amount to aggressions on the rights of those States whose citizens are injured by them, may be considered as another probable source of hostility."[31] Madison saw bills of attainder, ex post facto laws, and laws impairing the obligation of contract as "contrary to the first principles of social compact and to every principle of sound legislation."[32] It was "fluctuating policy" in this regard that, he thought, had prompted the people to reform the Articles of Confederation.

Similarly, the commerce clause was included in the Constitution to give the federal government a *negative* check on state control of interstate trade.[33] If individual states were allowed to impose duties on goods in interstate commerce, the terms of trade would be "artificially" altered and the incentive to seek out positive-sum transactions reduced. The Founding Fathers had seen the results of allowing state regulation and hoped to prevent it.

> The necessity of superintending authority over the reciprocal trade of confederated States has been illustrated by other examples as well as our own. In Switzerland, where the Union is so very slight, each canton is obliged to allow to merchandises a passage through its jurisdiction into

other cantons, without an augmentation of the tolls. In Germany it is a law of the empire that the princes and states shall not lay tolls or customs on the bridges, rivers, or passages, without the consent of the emperor and the diet; though it appears from a quotation in an antecedent paper that the practice in this, as in many other instances in that confederacy, has not followed the law, and had produced there the mischiefs which have been foreseen here.[34]

Tolls on interstate commerce infringed the rights of property owners to do what they pleased with their property as long as their actions did not injure innocent third parties.

And finally, the proposition that persons could not be deprived of "life, liberty or property, without due process of law" was designed to ensure that these rights could not be transferred away from individuals except as provided for by the Constitution. In including the compensation clause of the Fifth Amendment,

> there can be little doubt that the Framers thought the protection of property rights a very important thing indeed, and that a reading of the Constitution which would render the compensation clause a dead letter would be contrary to their intentions. It is, however, equally plain that the Framers were neither blind worshipers of the market nor principled opponents of active government in all its forms . . . Our fundamental problem is the same as theirs: to reconcile the competing demands of state and market in a way that gives absolute priority to neither.[35]

Police powers were granted to the government to carry out certain protective and productive functions, but these powers were not to be used without due process. As long as this process was followed, the constitutional contract would be working to sanctify private rights. Due process clearly placed restraints on the taking of private property by the government at both the federal (Fifth Amendment) and, much later, the state (Fourteenth Amendment) levels.

FIVE

⟷

Interpreting the Contract

The Constitution that the independent colonies adopted represented a significant break from the past. It did embody much English thought in its attempts to limit government but specified those limits more clearly than any previous document. The English had done a better job than others of developing private rights, but even there no clear-cut limits existed to prevent transfer activity. The colonists had learned that there were two threats to private rights: direct taking by other individuals and indirect taking through the coercive power of government itself. In order to prevent the former, a government was established; in order to prevent that government from growing into Leviathan, specific limitations were written into the Constitution.

Once the Constitution was ratified, the game began under a new set of rules. But disputes over the precise meaning of the new rules of the game had to be resolved. During the last years of the eighteenth century and the first half of the nineteenth century, several issues of immense importance had to be settled, including the struggle for an independent judiciary, the delineation of private rights under the contract clause, and the specification of government authority to intervene in economic operations. The Supreme Court in general and Chief Justice John Marshall in particular played key roles in this process.

THE SUPREMACY OF THE COURT

Surprisingly enough, the Constitution did not empower one tribunal to interpret disputes arising under the document: Article VI does provide that "this Constitution, and the Laws of the United States which shall be made in Pursuance thereof . . . shall be the Supreme Law of the Land; and the Judges in every State shall be bound thereby, any Thing in the Constitution or Laws of any State to the Contrary notwithstanding." The states' righters had, of course, thought that this settled the issue, but the Federalists saw a broader role for federal courts—at least with respect to acts of Congress and conflicting opinions between state courts. It is unlikely, however, that either group expected the Supreme Court to assume the interpretive power it eventually did. Article I, Section 8 gave Congress the power "to constitute Tribunals inferior to the Supreme Court" and Article III delineated specific cases where the federal judiciary was to act. But the Judiciary Act of 1789, passed during the first session of Congress, opened the door for federal supremacy by allowing appeal from state courts to the Supreme Court whenever state courts: "(1) ruled against the constitutionality of a federal treaty or law; (2) ruled in favor of the validity of a state act which had been challenged as contrary to the Constitution . . . ; or (3) ruled against a right or privilege claimed under the Constitution or federal law."[1] As cases were adjudicated, it became increasingly clear that this act formed the backbone of federal supremacy.

Passage of the 1789 act, however, did not automatically thrust the Supreme Court into the position of ultimate tribunal on constitutional issues. In fact, during its first three years of existence, the court did not rule on a single case. This changed during the final decade of the eighteenth century as lawyers came to know the system and as justices began to assert the authority granted under the act. The first Supreme Court ruling espousing the supremacy of federal law and federal judicial power came in 1793, but before that, lower federal courts had declared state laws unconstitutional. In 1791, the U.S. Circuit Court for Connecticut ruled that a state law abrogating the obligation to pay to British creditors interest accrued during the war was unconstitutional. A similar ruling from a Rhode Island Circuit Court in 1792 helped lay the groundwork for *Chisholm* v. *Georgia* (1793) and *Ware* v. *Hylton* (1796), two of the earliest Supreme Court cases declaring state laws unconstitutional. *Chisholm* v. *Georgia*, the more famous of the two, involved a dispute between a British creditor and the state of Georgia. Although the court's ruling in favor of Chisholm eventually led to passage of the Eleventh Amendment, which provided that "the judicial power of the United States shall not be construed to extend to any suit in law or equity, commenced or prosecuted against one of the United States by Citizens of another State, or by Citizens or Subjects of any Foreign State," it also provided a precedent for Supreme Court supremacy.

The power of the court gradually increased, but the real change came in 1801 with the appointment of John Marshall as chief justice. Interestingly enough, Marshall's appointment came only after John Jay declined reappointment to the court because "I left the bench perfectly convinced that under a system so defective it would not obtain the energy, weight, and dignity which are essential to its affording due support to the national government, nor acquire the public confidence and respect which, as the last resort of the justice of the nation, it should possess."[2] Marshall's years as chief justice were to change this image.

From the outset Marshall asserted the court's authority as guardian of the Constitution and tribunal of last resort. In three cases during 1801 (*Talbot* v. *Seeman, Wilson* v. *Mason*, and *United States* v. *Schooner Peggy*), Marshall's determination to establish the interpretive and appellate powers of the court became apparent. Mason's lawyers contended that the Supreme Court had no jurisdiction in *Wilson* v. *Mason* because Kentucky and Virginia had agreed that land title cases between the states could not be appealed beyond local district courts. In addressing them Marshall made his position clear:

> The constitution of the United States, to which the parties to this compact have assented, gave jurisdiction to the federal courts in controversies between citizens of different states. The same constitution vested in this court an appellate jurisdiction in all cases where original jurisdiction was given to the inferior courts, with only "such exceptions and under such regulations as the congress shall make" . . . If then the compact between Virginia and Kentucky was even susceptible of the construction contended for, that construction could only be maintained on the principle that the legislature of any two states might, by agreement between themselves, annul the constitution of the United States.[3]

His court was indeed supreme.

As Marshall's tenure lengthened, his decisions solidified the supremacy of the Constitution. In *Marbury* v. *Madison* (1803), one of his most famous opinions, Marshall used his power to confront the rising tide of Jeffersonian democracy, which was designed to limit the authority of the federal government. At issue was President Jefferson's power to withhold a justice of the peace commission issued by his predecessor, President Adams, and the Supreme Court's ability to issue a mandamus directing delivery of the commission. Tactfully, Marshall argued that the Adams's appointment was a contract and therefore could not be violated. But he also refused to issue the writ of mandamus on the grounds that the clause in the Judiciary Act of 1789 that authorized the court to issue such writs was unconstitutional. In so doing, he disarmed his Jeffersonian attackers and struck down the only act of Congress to be nullified by the court during the first half of the nineteenth century. Other cases involving judicial review continued to come before the Marshall court, including *United States* v. *Peters* (1809), *Martin* v. *Hunter's Lessee* (1816), *McCulloch* v. *Maryland* (1819), and *Cohens* v. *Virginia* (1821). The decisions in these cases reflect Marshall's contention that "if the legislatures of the several states may, at will, annul the judgments of the courts of the United States, and destroy the rights acquired under those judgments, the Constitution itself becomes a solemn mockery."[4] The energy, weight, and dignity to which Jay referred changed during the first third of the nineteenth century; so much so that Chief Justice Earl Warren stated: "Perhaps the greatest contribution he [Marshall] made to our system of jurisprudence was the establishment of the independent judiciary through the principle of judicial review."[5]

THE CONTRACT CLAUSE

If this was Marshall's greatest contribution, then his interpretations of the contract clause surely must have run a close second. As with judicial review, cases involving the sanctity of contracts were in the federal courts before Marshall assumed the chief justiceship. Disputes arising from debtor-creditor claims between citizens of the United States and Great Britain provided the first test of the contract clause. Since the treaty with Great Britain following the Revolutionary War specified that all such claims should be honored, state laws passed under the Articles of Confederation or the Constitution that relieved American creditors of debts were ruled unconstitutional under the contract clause. *Champion* v. *Casey* (1792), and *Ware* v. *Hylton* (1796) are excellent examples of early use of this constitutional provision. The full power of the contract clause, however, was manifested during the reign of the great chief justice. Leonard Baker, in one of the most complete discussions of Marshall's support of the sanctity of contracts, notes both the significance and the probable origins of Marshall's concept of contracts:

> Enforcement of contractual arrangements had been a concern of the federal courts for years. One of Marshall's first cases as a Chief Justice had involved

landholdings and the contractual arrangements over who was the actual
owner. The issue has developed through the western land disputes, the ships
seizure cases, and a number of others. What was evolving was a law of contracts, of property. The theme was that when a man earned something,
neither a person nor a government should be able to take it from him. One
purpose of government is, in fact, to protect a man from assaults on his
property, whether those assaults be by marauders, neighbors, or an arm of
government itself. The John Marshall who had grown up on the frontier,
who had seen the young America split from England because American
property was being confiscated in the form of taxation without representation, the John Marshall who had seen the revolutionaries in France usurp
property before not only an impotent but a cooperating government, this
John Marshall was well aware that government must protect a man from
theft by his government.[6]

One of the earliest and most famous Marshall court cases applying the
contract clause was *Fletcher* v. *Peck* (1810; sometimes called the Yazoo
Land Case), which involved an attempt by the Georgia legislature to
rescind a land grant made in a previous legislative session because of
fraud in the original action. Writing for the majority, Chief Justice
Marshall concluded that since third parties had now entered into
contracts involving the land, those contracts could not be abrogated. He
emphasized that "it may well be doubted whether the nature of society
and of the government does not prescribe some limits to the legislature
power; and if any be prescribed, where are they to be found, if the
property of an individual, fairly and honestly acquired, may be seized
without compensation?"[7] In this case, Marshall's decision relied partially
on the general principle of vested rights and partially on specific
prohibitions against impairing the obligation of contracts. He was
concerned not just with the immediate dispute before the court but with
the long-run implications of contractual interference. By applying the
contract clause to "contracts of every description," Marshall was able to
"build the Constitution into a bulwark for the protection of the property
owner. Moved by such a purpose, he no doubt believed that it was
as essential—perhaps more so—to keep government from disturbing
economic arrangements as it was to hold private persons to their
agreements."[8]

The power of the contract clause to limit the ability of governments to
alter property rights was expanded in *Dartmouth College* v. *Woodward*
(1819). At issue was the power of the state of New Hampshire to alter the

charter granted by George III to Dartmouth College in 1769. The court ruled that when a government granted an article of incorporation, such a grant was to be viewed as a contract and immune to governmental interference thereafter, even if, as in this case, the granting government no longer ruled the territory. A lawyer for the state of New Hampshire contended that the contract clause was intended "to protect private rights of property and embraces all contracts relating to private property" but not "to limit the power of the states, in relation to their own public officers or servants, or their own civil institutions . . . nor grants of power and authority, by a state to individuals, to be exercised for purposes merely public."[9] But Marshall's contention that "contracts of every description" were embraced by the clause did not waver: "It can require no argument to prove that the circumstances of this case constitute a contract."[10] Marshall's broad interpretation of the concept of contract further supported the idea that the actions states could take with respect to private property were limited. The actual restriction, however, on the ability of the states to alter corporate charters was modified somewhat by Justice Joseph Story's concurring opinion that states could reserve the right, in future charters, to repeal or alter the powers granted corporations.

Although the contract clause was used numerous times early in the nineteenth century to prevent legislative action that significantly altered rights, the effectiveness of this barrier was gradually diminished as a result of Supreme Court decisions relating to the "bankruptcy cases." *Sturges* v. *Crowninshield* (1819) negated a New York law that gave relief to debtors on the grounds that such relief impaired the obligation of contracts and was therefore unconstitutional under Article I, Section 10. Two constitutional provisions were at stake in the case: the contract clause and the power granted to Congress to pass "uniform Laws on the subject of Bankruptcies throughout the United States" (Article I, Section 8). Concluding that the latter clause did not preclude states from passing similar legislation as long as it was consistent with federal laws, Marshall asked, "Does the law of New York, which is pleaded in this case, impair the obligation of contracts, within the meaning of the constitution of the United States?"[11] In another ruling, he concluded:

> It is not true that the parties have in view only the property in possession when the contract is formed, or that its obligation does not extend to future acquisitions. Industry, talents, and integrity, constitute a fund which is as

confidently entrusted as property itself. Future acquisitions are, therefore, liable for contracts; and to release them from this liability impairs their obligation.[12]

In the ensuing years several other bankruptcy cases came before the Marshall court; the decision in *Ogden* v. *Saunders* (1827) was the most significant. The law in question in this case differed from the earlier New York statute in that it applied only to contracts entered into after the law was passed. In a four to three decision, the majority of the court argued that such a law became part of the contract and hence did not violate the constitutional provision prohibiting the impairment of the obligations of contracts. The case is of interest for several reasons. This was the only substantive case during Marshall's tenure as chief justice that he was in a minority. Second, the ruling in the case reversed earlier decisions. Immediately following *Sturges* v. *Crowninshield*, Marshall had reiterated his position by stating that "the circumstances of the state law, under which the debt was attempted to be discharged, having been passed before the debt was contracted, made no difference in the application of the principle."[13] The most important aspect of the *Ogden* v. *Saunders* decision, however, was that it marked the turning point in the use of the contract clause as a barrier to transfers. Although this decision was crucial to bankruptcy legislation, it also significantly altered the ability of the Constitution to restrict legislative action. In effect, this decision allowed the government to alter any property rights involved in contractual exchange as long as that alteration occurred before the contract was entered into. Thus the freedom of property owners to use their property as they saw fit was appreciably reduced; perhaps more important, the benefits to transfer activity appreciably increased. Chief Justice Marshall saw the far-reaching implications: "Thus, one of the most important features in the constitution of the United States, one which the state of the times most urgently required, one on which the good and wise reposed confidently for securing the prosperity and harmony of our citizens, would lie prostrate, and be construed into an inanimate, inoperative, unmeaning clause."[14] In his dissent he went on to expound his Lockean views:

> As we have no evidence of the surrender, or of the restoration of the right; as this operation of surrender and restoration would be an idle and useless ceremony, the rational inference seems to be, that neither has ever been made; that individuals do not derive from government their right to con-

tract, but bring that right with them into society; that obligation is not conferred on contracts by positive law, but is intrinsic, and is conferred by the act of the parties. This results from the right which every man retains, to acquire property, to dispose of that property according to his own judgment, and to pledge himself for a future act. These rights are not given by society, but are brought to it.[15]

He continued by recalling the tenor of the Constitutional Convention itself and the period around the Revolution.

The power of changing the relative situation of debtor and creditor, of interfering with contracts, a power which comes home to every man, touches the interest of all, and controls the conduct of every individual in those things which he supposes to be proper for his own exclusive management, had been used to such an excess by the State legislatures, as to break in upon the ordinary intercourse of society, and destroy all confidence between man and man. The mischief had become so great, so alarming, as not only to impair commercial intercourse, and threaten the existence of credit, but to sap the morals of the people, and destroy the sanctity of private faith. To guard against the continuance of the evil was an object of deep interest with all the truly wise, as well as the virtuous, of this great community, and was one of the important benefits expected from a reform of the government.[16]

In Marshall's mind the *Ogden* v. *Saunders* decision greatly reduced these benefits of the Constitution. In one of the most comprehensive books on the contract clause, Benjamin Wright states that had Marshall's opinion in *Ogden* v. *Saunders* "been that of the majority, the decision . . . would have been as great a limitation upon state legislative power as any of his period, perhaps the most sweeping."[17]

THE COMMERCE CLAUSE

Although the effectiveness of the contract clause in limiting transfer activity was declining by very early in the nineteenth century, the court's decisions regarding states' rights to regulate economic activity, especially commerce, were countering this loss by reducing the ability of government to bestow special favors and privileges. *McCullough* v. *Maryland*, besides its importance for judicial review, limited the taxation powers of the states. The case concerned the power of the states to tax the U.S. Bank and thus prevent its operation within their borders. Said Chief

Justice Marshall, "That the power of taxing it [the bank] by the States may be exercised so as to destroy it, is too obvious to be denied."[18] The constitutional power of taxation granted to the states was not doubted, but the potential impact of such power on the ability of Congress to do what was "necessary and proper" was obvious. Because of the difficulty of distinguishing between "what is an abuse and what is a legitimate use of power,"[19] Marshall totally prohibited the states from taxing federal institutions.

Later rulings more directly restricted states under the commerce clause. In *Gibbons* v. *Ogden* (1824), which dealt with the power of New York to grant monopoly rights to steamship companies, the court held that Congress's power to "regulate commerce . . . among the several states" meant that such monopoly rights were invalid. Furthermore, "Marshall declared the validity of the Interstate Commerce Clause in giving the power to regulate interstate trade solely to the Federal government, and by proscribing the obstructive actions of individual states he helped to create the legal conditions that would permit the emergence of a broad national market."[20] *Brown* v. *Maryland* (1827) continued the quest for national control of interstate trade when the chief justice applied the commerce clause to prevent the state of Maryland from imposing taxes on goods imported into the state. Marshall contended that such a tax was unconstitutional if the goods remained in the same form as they were imported. Like his contract clause decisions, Marshall's opinions concerning the commerce clause tended to emphasize the sovereignty of the nation relative to that of the states and to constrain the ability of both state and federal governments to alter the structure of privately held rights. During Marshall's incumbency the court declared statutes of over half the states unconstitutional, and many of these declarations came under the commerce clause. But although nothing in these Supreme Court decisions prevented the federal government from regulating commerce, for the first century of the nation's existence the Congress did not act in this arena. The commerce clause was a negative check on state interference with interstate commerce rather than a positive guide for federal intervention. In fact, before the Civil War, the sole use of the commerce clause by the Supreme Court was to negate state statutes.

Although this implies that early nineteenth-century transfers of income, wealth, and rights were difficult to obtain through the federal government, some transfers were carried out. The U.S. economy was not completely laissez-faire.[21] Productive activity dominated transfer activity during the first three quarters of the century, but some transfer activity undoubtedly occurred. The Constitution significantly constrained such transfers, but several areas of potential government action were available. The two most significant were tariffs and subsidies for transportation improvements, including the right of eminent domain. Trade policy was a major political issue both before and immediately after the Revolution. Although the Constitution abolished internal trade barriers, it did not prohibit federal enactment of external barriers. There were few in Congress during its early sessions who advocated absolutely no government intervention, but there was general agreement that "one function of government should be to stimulate all nationally beneficial occupations and enterprises."[22] Congress responded by passing numerous tariff laws throughout the nineteenth century; such laws did represent an opportunity for transfers of income from one segment of the society to another.[23] Public assistance for transportation was another potential area for major transfers. Since no constitutional clause prohibited such action, about three-fourths of the total investment in canal construction before the Civil War came from government sources.[24] Government aid to railroads did not constitute a large portion of total investment but was still significant.[25]

In addition to transfer activity at the federal level, state and local governments were involved in altering the property rights structure, with most regulation between 1800 and 1830 undertaken by the states:[26]

> The multitude of state laws prescribing specific varieties of governmental intervention with business activity, together with the much *smaller body* of federal legislation restricting entrepreneurial freedom, indicate clearly that the American enterprise system in the Age of Washington did not operate under a system of *laissez-faire*. Commerce was restricted by state tariff laws before the adoption of the Constitution and by a federal tariff system after the new government came into operation. (emphasis added)[27]

Here again transportation was one of the dominant areas of intervention, with states owning roads, canals, and railroads. States also passed legislation regulating the quality of commodities produced within the state, fixing interest charges on debts, and in certain cases setting wages, fees, and even prices of some products.[28] Much emphasis has been placed on the precedent of state regulation,[29] and its importance should not be ignored. One important constraint, however, on state regulatory activity lessened the desire of the state legislatures to engage in transfer activity. To the extent that such activity lowered the return to engaging in productive activity, resources flowed out of the state. Thus any state that attempted large-scale transfers of rights might well have found itself at a severe competitive disadvantage with surrounding states that were not using their legislative powers to such ends.[30]

Therefore the magnitude of transfer activity at all levels of government during the first three-quarters of the nineteenth century should not be exaggerated. Says the legal historian Lawrence Friedman, "Despite all these examples of economic regulation, 19th-century government was no leviathan. Even in the large Eastern states, its hold over the economy was weak. Many programs must have existed only on paper. Many of the inspection laws, licensing laws, and laws about weights and measures were feeble and vapidly enforced."[31] Instead of taxes, states used fee systems to force users of services to pay for them. Cases like *McCulloch* v. *Maryland* limited state power to tax on the grounds that with such power came the power to destroy what was taxed. Even Harry Scheiber, who argues that governmental regulation had considerable precedent, agrees that "the heyday of expropriation as an instrument of public policy designed to subsidize private enterprise can probably be dated as beginning in the 1870's."[32] While arguing that the transformation in American law between 1780 and 1860 opened the door for redistribution, Morton J. Horwitz adds that revolutionary constitutional law was countering this transformation:

> By forging constitutional doctrines under the Contracts Clause barring retroactive laws and giving constitutional status to "vested rights," this line of intellectual development sought basically to limit the ability of the legal system—more specifically, of the legislature—to bring about redistributions of wealth. While the first tendency [changes in property and tort law] underlined and acknowledged the malleable—and hence political—character of law, the second sought to depoliticize the law and to insist upon its objective, neutral, and facilitative character.[33]

In the words of James Willard Hurst, the first three-quarters of the nineteenth century was characterized by a "release of energy."[34] Productive activity dominated transfer activity. President Jefferson's first message to Congress emphasized that "agriculture, manufactures, commerce, and navigation, the four pillars of our prosperity, are . . . most thriving when left most free to individual enterprise."[35] In one of the best examples of deregulation during the early years of the republic, the

Pennsylvania legislature refused to continue regulating bread prices partly on the grounds that it did "infringe the equality of rights established by the State Constitution."[36]

The role of the Marshall court in promoting this climate for productive activity cannot be denied. The chief justice and his fellows

> realized the corrupting nature of power, understood that as men enter government, learn to use its offices, see the results they can achieve, they begin to confuse their original obligations with their new purposes, their role as servants of the people with that of arbiters of the people's needs. This arrogance of government is what in a democracy must constantly be guarded against, and the role of guardians and protectors is the one that John Marshall and the Supreme Court he led were assuming.[37]

Thus Marshall established important bulwarks against transfer activity; the interpretations of his court protected property rights, limited the role of government, and generally allowed individuals to pursue positive-sum games.

SIX
$\longleftrightarrow$

The Seeds of Change

During the years immediately following Marshall's tenure as chief justice, Supreme Court interpretations of the Constitution did not change significantly. The protection given property rights and individual freedom of contract during the first 35 years of the nineteenth century was, if anything, expanded. Both the contract clause and the commerce clause of the Constitution continued to provide a foundation for a society that emphasized productive activity.

On the other hand, significant changes in American society laid a foundation for the alteration of the institutional structure. In terms of the proper limits for government, the social and political theories that became popular during the era of Jacksonian democracy were profoundly significant.

THE TANEY COURT

Although Roger Taney, chief justice of the Supreme Court from 1836 to 1864, was an ardent Jacksonian, his time on the court did not mark a significant departure from the rather strict constructionist doctrines of his predecessor, John Marshall. Thus this period was one of changing attitudes about government, but not one in which interpretations of the Constitution provided a substantial alteration in the returns to productive and transfer activity. These changing views were not reflected either in amendments to the Constitution or in substantial shifts in interpretation of that document. Transfer activity remained limited, and productive activity was encouraged.

There were, however, many attempts to change the Constitution; over four hundred amendments were proposed between 1804 and 1860,[1] but none was passed. Many people expected the Taney court to be much more receptive to the new thinking than it was. Taney's tenure, however, did not fulfill the expectations of his Democratic supporters, who contended that "his republican notions, together with those of his democratic associates, will produce a revolution in some important particulars in the doctrines heretofore advanced by the tribunal, over which he is called to preside, highly favorable to the independence of the States, and the substantial freedom of the people."[2] The relative stability of the Taney court can be seen in its interpretations of two important constitutional prohibitions of transfer activity, the contract clause and the commerce clause.

Despite the decision in *Ogden* v. *Saunders* (1827), which eventually nullified the contract clause as a limit on transfers, for a period of time the clause still served to check state laws that tried to limit freedom of contract. The Taney court did not choose to apply the *Ogden* v. *Saunders* doctrine but instead hearkened back to an earlier Marshall decision, *Sturges* v. *Crowninshield*, which prevented governmental interference in contracts. For instance, in *Bronson* v. *Kinzie* (1843) the court invalidated two Illinois laws that it said impaired the obligations of contracts by restricting foreclosure sales.

One change in the interpretation of the contract clause was significant, although some implications of the decision have been ignored. In 1837, in *Charles River Bridge* v. *Warren Bridge*, Taney and his associates ruled that charter grants must be interpreted narrowly. At issue was the right of Massachusetts to grant a charter for a second bridge over the Charles River. The Charles River Bridge Company contended that the charter allowing construction of a second bridge not far from its own violated the original charter. The Taney court ruled in favor of the Warren Bridge, stating that "in charters of this description, no rights are taken from the public, or given to the corporation, beyond those which the words of the charter by their natural and proper construction, purport to convey."[3] This opinion limited the stricter construction of the contract clause in *Dartmouth College*, but it was also consistent with an 1830 Marshall court decision that upheld the power of a state to tax corporations even if the corporate charter did not specify the right to tax. Said Chief Justice Marshall, "The Plaintiffs find great difficulty in showing that the charter contains a promise, *either expressed or implied*, not to tax the bank [emphasis added]."[4] Conservatives on the court feared the *Charles River Bridge* decision would eventually erode the doctrine of judicial review as a protection of private property from legislative encroachment, but "Taney and his associates proved to be little inclined to disturb Marshall's doctrines concerning the relationship between state legislation and private contractual rights between individuals."[5] In fact, during the 28 years of Taney's term, the contract clause was invoked eighteen times to strike down state laws, compared with eight times during Marshall's 34 years.[6] Moreover, after the *Charles River Bridge* decision it became clear that well-specified corporate charters removed doubts about the terms of the contract.

Another aspect of the *Charles River Bridge* v. *Warren Bridge* case, however, is often overlooked by legal scholars. One implication of *Dartmouth College* was that contracts between the state and private parties were inviolable, thus opening the door for the granting of monopoly privileges. Such privileges in essence transfer to recipients of the monopoly the right to monopoly profits and deny consumers the right to contract with other producers of the good or service. The interpretation of the contract clause in *Charles River Bridge*, however, simply allowed any benefits from such monopoly privileges to be eroded by further state action. This, combined with Marshall's decision in *Gibbons* v. *Ogden*, erected a substantial hurdle for states' desiring to issue monopoly grants. Of course, states were able to circumvent these interpretations to a certain extent by writing charters including the specific monopoly provisions they desired; nonetheless, the strict contractarian approach of the court did limit transfer activity.

There were also some changes in the interpretation of the commerce clause, but, like the contract clause, these did not significantly depart from the Marshall decisions. The Taney court did not alter the limitations on the states' powers to interfere with interstate commerce that Marshall had laid down in *Gibbons* v. *Ogden*. Since this case was crucial in restricting the power of the states to grant monopoly privileges and to interfere with mutually agreed trades, the adherence of the court to the general constructs of this doctrine made state transfer activity much less profitable.

The Taney court did allow some expansion of the police power of the states and argued that in the absence of direct action by the federal government, the states could make decisions that had incidental impacts on interstate commerce. For instance, *New York* v. *Miln* (1837) exemplified the growing attitude that there were cases where the police power of the state could be used to promote safety, health, convenience of trade, and general welfare at the expense of free interstate trade. In this license case the court ruled that taxes on liquor imported from other states had only an "incidental effect" on interstate commerce and therefore did not violate the commerce clause. Such legislation was justified through the police power granted to the states. In addition, Taney believed that states had the right to regulate commerce as long as there was an absence of federal legislation in the area. This concept of concurrent powers eventually led to the doctrine of "selective exclusiveness," which gave states authority over certain aspects of commerce even though they might involve interstate trade. Nevertheless neither the expansion of the police power nor the allowance of some state control over interstate commerce caused an immediate increase in transfer activity. The constitutional interpretations on which the rise in transfer activity were based did not come till after the Civil War. But the seeds for this transfer activity were being sown in the ideology of the Jacksonian Democrats.

CHANGING VIEWS

The era of Jacksonian democracy was a period of rapid economic and social change. Real per capita income doubled in less than fifty years. Expansion of the frontier allowed the geographic mobility of labor and capital and changed social relations among those factors. The Eastern Seaboard, previously the locus of economic and political activity, found its position usurped by the dynamic forces of the growing West. The population of the United States grew from 9,618,000 in 1820 to 23,261,000 by 1850.[7] Moreover, significant changes occurred in transportation and communication. In 1800 it took Jefferson nearly two weeks to travel from Monticello to New York, but by 1830 the travel time between Charleston and New York had been reduced to five days and by 1860 the journey from Rock Island on the Mississippi River to New York required only two days. Increased use of the telegraph reduced the cost of transmitting information. Furthermore, the society underwent a transition from a predominately agrarian to an industrial society. In 1810 nearly two million workers were engaged in farm labor while fewer than a half million were engaged in nonfarm labor. By 1840 the ratio of farm to nonfarm laborers had fallen to approximately 1.6 to 1.0 and by 1880 the labor force was equally divided.[8] Such changes resulted in wealth instability and increased the demand for transfers.

Besides the changes in the distribution of wealth, there were important alterations in basic attitudes that affected the evolution of the institutional structure. First, the perception of the nature of man was changing. Second, expansion of the franchise was altering the concept of democracy and causing a shift toward majority decisions. Third, equity was replacing efficiency as a measure of the working of markets. And finally, the view of natural rights was being revised.

Living in a growing economy meant more than an expanding opportunity to consume increasingly available goods and services. Because of the dynamic nature of the economy, the idea of progress overflowed into all aspects of American thinking. Americans came to assume that progress was inevitable in every aspect of the world around them. Even moral and intellectual progress was seen as a natural result of social growth. This progress was to allow man to rise above self-interest: "For Democracy is the cause of Humanity. It has faith in human nature. It believes in its essential equality and fundamental goodness . . . It is, moreover, a cheerful creed, a creed of high hope and universal love, noble and ennobling."[9] In this view of democracy, limitations on government were not necessary. All that was necessary for good government was to secure broad participation in the decision-making process so that class privilege would not assert itself; the result would be collective action in the social interest. This contrasts sharply with the sentiments about mankind expressed in the *Federalist Papers* and other writings of that period. As Madison said, "If men were angels, no government would be necessary. If angels were to govern men, neither external nor internal controls on government would be necessary."[10] Because Madison and others did not believe that men were angels, they attempted to construct controls on government. To many thinkers and writers of the Jacksonian era these controls were a sign of elitism, and their removal would ensure greater participation in collective decisions and hence better government. Since mankind was intrinsically good, the controls on government were not necessary as long as participation by the populace was widespread.

This desire to expand the role of the general public in the political process naturally led to expansion of the franchise. When the Constitution was framed, the freehold qualification was not particularly restrictive because a large portion of the population consisted of landowners and farmers. But as population density increased and as industrialization reduced the proportion of the labor force in farming, the percentage of adult males owning real property decreased. In Rhode Island, for example, at the time of the Revolution between 50 and 75 percent of the adult males met the freehold qualification. By 1790 the percentage of freeholders in Providence had fallen to 33 percent, and in 1841 only about 40 percent of the state's adult male population met the ownership requirements.[11] Expanding the franchise was thus essential to maintaining a government based on the consent of the governed.

Although this rise of democracy and the expansion of the franchise were appropriate for the changes in social structure, they also resulted in an increased reliance on majority rule that was not conducive to a continuation of a society living under a government restricted by constitutional limits. The problem lay in the confusion between expansion of the franchise to include a wider spectrum of society and the belief that a simple majority had the right to make all decisions. The extension of suffrage to include more individuals bound by the constitutional contract added legitimacy to the protective and productive decisions of the state. But allowing majority rule to dictate any changes in the rules of the game desired by a majority opened the door for the tyranny so feared by Madison. Again and again writers in popular journals characterized the choice as one of majority versus minority rule.[12] When the majority was not allowed to do what it willed, this was taken as obvious evidence that aristocratic elements were in power. Although constitutional limitations on majority decisions undoubtedly served to protect the class privileges of certain individuals,[13] the principle of limiting the "tyranny of the majority" was important for all classes of society. In reacting against what was perceived as oppression by those who had privilege and wealth, the Jacksonians did not seem to recognize the potential for oppression in a society where there were no rights not subject to alteration by the majority. A clear case can be made for expanding the franchise while maintaining well-defined limits on the ability of the people or their elected representatives to alter fundamental rights. Most Jacksonians, however, did not make this distinction.[14]

Other changes were occurring in attitudes toward economic growth and the sharing of gains from that growth. During the early years of federation, increases in income were seen as a measure of one's social contribution rather than as evidence of venality. However, the rising tide of egalitarianism during the Jacksonian era meant that, in the eyes of some, any gain by one person had to be at the expense of another.

> For whatever exalts the few, humbles the many; and luxury and splendor grow from poverty and want. Some must be poor, that others may be rich. And wherever we find the few possessed of excessive riches, we find, as a consequence, the many reduced to excessive poverty. For riches can no more exist without poverty than mountains without valleys. If there were not a single rich man in the world, there would be no less wealth in the world than there is now; but then it would be spread equally over the whole surface of society, diffusing equal abundance, comfort, and happiness among all.[15]

One can categorize viewpoints concerning the distribution of gains into two basic camps: those who believe that market transactions (trades) result in positive-sum games making both parties to the transactions better off and those who believe that such trades are zero or negative sum so that one party gains at the expense of the other. For the former, resentment of another's income is pure envy since that income does not make others poorer. For the latter, however, wealth is limited and dividing it more evenly does not reduce the total amount available. The Founding Fathers were more closely aligned with the positive-sum camp, but attitudes toward wealth accumulation underwent substantial change during the antebellum period. This meant that government redistributive programs were much easier to justify. If the rich became wealthy at the expense of the poor, then the moral argument for coercive redistribution was much more powerful than if increased wealth did not mean a decrease in someone else's income.

Finally, there was a transformation in the minds of some social theorists about the composition of natural rights. Previously natural rights were primarily rights to oneself and to all with which one's labor was mixed, but the concept came to mean a right to an equal share of all property. Thomas Skidmore, in his "Plan for Equalizing Property," suggests that

> man's natural right to an equal portion of property is indisputable. His artificial right, or right in society, is not less so. For it is not to be said that any power has any right to make our artificial rights unequal any more than it has to make our natural rights unequal. And inasmuch as a man in a state of nature would have a right to resist, even in the extremity of death, his fellow or his fellows, whatever might be their number, who should under- take to give him less of the property common to all than they take each to

themselves; so also has man now, in society, the same right to resist a similar wrong done him. Thus, today, if property has been made equal among all present, right would have taken place among them.[16]

If the Constitution were a document designed to protect one's vested or natural rights as conceived by Skidmore, a significant alteration in the role of government would be called for. Under the new view the state would be actively involved in creating social equality, a function of government not envisioned by the Founding Fathers.

These shifts in opinion were crucial in the origins of the transfer society. On the demand side, the dynamics of growth caused significant changes in the distribution of wealth. Hence individuals turned to the government to maintain their wealth positions. On the supply side, ideology changed in favor of transfer activity. An explicit faith in the goodness of man and human progress made government seem much more a vehicle of social reform than a potential agent of oppression. The rise of egalitarianism led to a belief in the propriety of income redistribution measures through the coercive power of government, and the increased reliance on majority rule facilitated the use of this power. The perception of all economic transactions as zero-sum games promoted negative-sum games in the governmental arena. These changes took several decades to come to fruition, but they led to the birth of the transfer society in the postbellum era.

SEVEN
←——————→

The Rise of Transfers

I select this date [1898] because . . . that year was the turning
point in our political and constitutional history. Down to that
date, the movement of that history had been an almost un-
broken march in the direction of a more and more perfect
individual liberty and immunity against the powers of government, and a more and more complete and efficient organization
and operation of sovereignty back of both government and
defining and guaranteeing individual liberty. From that date to
the present the movement has been in the contrary direction,
until now there remains hardly an individual immunity against
governmental power which may not be set aside by government, at its own will and discretion, with or without reason, as
government itself may determine.

John W. Burgess
Recent Changes in American
Constitutional Theory

When John Burgess wrote this statement in 1923, it is unlikely that he
realized the full extent of its validity or foresaw the extent to which the
role of government would increase. Although some coercive transfers of
rights took place in the first half of the nineteenth century, many other
attempts at transfers were unsuccessful. Laws regulating pay, working
hours, prices, rates, and general contractual conditions were ruled
unconstitutional by the Supreme Court. The due process clause of the
Fifth Amendment was used to protect life, liberty, and property from
the police powers of the state. Before 1850 it was used primarily in
criminal cases to ensure certain procedural rights to defendants. Thereafter, however, the clause began to acquire substance as the Supreme
Court began considering the constitutionality of cases on the basis of
whether they infringed the rights of property and contract. The court's
decision that these rights were inviolable was evident in such cases as
Wynehamer v. *New York* (1856) in which the New York Court of Appeals
ruled a law regulating the manufacture of liquor unconstitutional and

Hepburn v. *Griswold* (1870) in which Chief Justice Salmon Chase claimed that the Legal Tender Act of 1862, which made greenbacks legal tender for debts, was unconstitutional because it was contrary to due process and violated the obligation of contracts. Again it is evident that the emphasis was on productive activity promoted by private property rights.

Even in considering property rights in humans (*Dred Scott* v. *Sanford*, 1857), Chief Justice Taney ruled that the Fifth Amendment prohibited the federal government from imposing restrictions on property in slaves. Whatever the morality involved, this decision did provide protection against transfers of rights. As discussed in chapter 2, rights must be legitimate before it can be argued that coercive transfers are morally wrong. The issue of legitimacy of rights is one that society must resolve.[1] If existing rights are clearly perceived as illegitimate, coercion may be brought to bear, as it was in the Civil War, to resolve the issue. Despite the slavery issue's position as the major constitutional crisis of our history, its impact was minimal in terms of continued transfer activity. The legitimacy of certain rights was questioned; a war was fought to resolve the issue; and economic activity then continued under the previous ground rules except that certain property rights were held by different owners. Although the Civil War did not lead to significant transfer activity, we must again caution that resolving a legitimacy issue can precipitate negative-sum activity.

Other evidence that productive rather than transfer activity was encouraged is found in the government's policy on the disposal of public land. Although the movement of land from public to private ownership might be considered a transfer, private ownership is necessary to promote positive-sum games. The Homestead Acts, the Timber-Stone Act, and other similar legislation, as well as the large land grants to the transcontinental railroads, were designed to shift land from the public domain into private hands. Private individuals were encouraged to promote the "release of energy" by developing and exploiting the vast natural resources of the western United States.

And finally, profits earned through the private enterprise system were emphasized and considered good for the individual, as well as for the country as a whole. In Hurst's words, "pursuit of profit not only justified doing ordinary competitive damage to a market rival, but was a business firm's whole legal excuse for being."[2] In fact, according to a Michigan court, "a business corporation is organized and carried on primarily for the profit of the stockholders . . . It is not within the lawful powers of a board of directors to shape and conduct the affairs of a corporation for the merely incidental benefit of shareholders and for the primary purpose of benefiting others."[3]

According to Burgess, the emphasis on productive activity changed during the last quarter of the nineteenth century. When did this change occur, why did it occur, what legal changes allowed the rise of transfers, and what evidence is there of transfer activity?

POSTBELLUM ECONOMIC CONDITIONS

From the end of the Civil War to the early twentieth century, U.S. economic growth resulted in a threefold increase in per capita output, or a rate of growth of over 1.5 percent per year. Deflation dominated prices from 1865 to the turn of the century, allowing for real as well as nominal growth. All, however, was not rosy. Money wages, which either remained constant or declined, caused discontent among workers. Debtors, especially in the farm sector, suffered as prices for outputs fell. Furthermore, as the market economy expanded and individuals became more interdependent, the effects of aggregate fluctuations became more widespread. If declining demand in one sector created unemployment, the effects were felt in other sectors as the spending of those unemployed decreased. Major depressions in 1873–1878, 1882–1885, and 1892–1894 seemed "to obscure long-term trends. In a rapidly expanding economy, people are prone to take periods of increasing output for granted and to be deeply concerned about years of disappointing increases or actual decreases."[4]

Although people were concerned about the rate of growth during this period, they also seemed to become more concerned about the distribution of income resulting from that growth. This was seen as the era of the robber barons, with names such as Carnegie, Morgan, and Rockefeller dominating many a discussion of social problems. Big business meant big money, and to the average worker it appeared that the wealthy capitalists were taking more than their fair share. Acceptance of this conclusion was common during the late nineteenth century. Monopoly, thought to be in its heyday, prompted such legislation as the Sherman Antitrust Act (1890) and the Clayton Act (1914). The agricultural sector was particularly vocal, with repeated complaints of monopoly power by the railroads, of price fixing by middlemen, and of imperfections in capital markets. The combination of these complaints led many to conclude that this period was characterized by exploitation of the masses.

Data on total assets held by the top wealthholders suggest that distribution had become more uneven following the Revolution. Lindert and Williamson conclude that America's richest 10 percent increased their share of total wealth between 1776 and 1860 "by as much as 15 percentage points."[5] During the 1860s, however, there was a leveling of the distribution, and the period from 1860 to 1929 was a high, uneven plateau of wealth inequality.[6] It would appear, therefore, that the maldistribution perceived during the last quarter of the nineteenth century was a result of antebellum rather than postbellum growth.

Data on income and monopoly, however, do not support the progressive era's allegations of concentration. According to Gray and Peterson:

> In the period from 1840 to 1900, the division of national income between labor and property owners (capital and natural resource suppliers) remained in a 70–30 ratio. Over the same time span, both capital and developed natural resources increased faster than the labor force. This means that labor incomes per unit of labor input rose compared with profits and interest per unit of property input.[7]

Unfortunately, data that would allow computation of the changes in income distribution do not exist. Undoubtedly some of those in the upper-income brackets were getting richer, but so were many individuals closer to the mean and median. With the relative size of the middle class increasing, it is unlikely that the income of any class declined absolutely. Moreover, on the monopoly issue, Douglass North estimates that even if the "excess profits of monopoly" had amounted to $400 million per year and if these had been redistributed across the population, per capita income would have increased by only two percent.[8] Another study of the Standard Oil Company concludes that the widely held belief in its predatory pricing policy is erroneous.[9] And finally, with respect to the complaints of farmers, evidence indicates that farm prices rose relative to nonfarm prices and remained constant relative to railroad rates.[10]

Although this casts some doubt on the conclusions of conventional history that the Gilded Age was one of concentration of power in the hands of a few wealthy individuals, we must remember that people's perception of the times is perhaps more important than what actually happened. The muckraker literature and complaints of deplorable working conditions suggest that the mood of the times was one of discontent with income distribution. This mood, coupled with earlier changes in attitudes during the Jacksonian period, greatly influenced institutional change during this period.

Urbanization also influenced this change. During the late nineteenth century, population in urban areas surpassed that in rural areas and the number of nonfarm workers that of farm workers. As people moved into more crowded conditions, the spillover effects on one's neighbors were much greater. The slums and filth resulting from the increased population density caused city dwellers to seek governmental redress of these problems. Intervention by the government into areas of spillovers brought an overall increase in nonmarket resource allocation relative to that of the market.

And finally, the closing of the American frontier that had been with us from the first settlement at Jamestown caused many changes. Cheap land, considered by some as a safety valve for many of our social problems, was mostly claimed either by private individuals or by governmental agencies. The rise in average population density from 10.6 persons per square mile in 1860 to 35.6 in 1920 tells most of the story. By the turn of the century most of the available land was less productive or less accessible. The possibility of establishing individual property rights over previously unclaimed natural resources diminished with each passing year and each new homestead. According to Lawrence Friedman, the impact of the closing of the frontier was psychological:

> What really passed was not the frontier, but the idea of the frontier. This inner sense of change was one of the most important influences on American law ... By 1900, if one can speak about so slippery a thing as dominant public opinion, that opinion saw a narrowing sky, a dead frontier, life as a struggle for position, competition as a zero-sum game, the economy as a pie to be divided, not a ladder stretching out beyond the horizon.[11]

The closing was hastened, of course, by the land reservation policy of the federal government during the late 1800s. The extensive use of resources that came with the release of energy during the first half of the century prompted the reservation of millions of acres of timber and grazing lands. The hope was to improve both efficiency and equity by substituting public for private allocation, but the success has been less than obvious.

The gains from economic growth in the postbellum period

are taken for granted, whereas the associated costs are emphasized and the business leaders of the day are cited with shame as "robber barons." Economic expansion and per capita income growth brought about a sweeping transformation in the structure of the economy and engendered disruption at the same time. Business fluctuations were sharp and frequent and generated high rates of unemployment. Innovations reduced costs but cast aside those whose businesses or skills tied them to outmoded processes. Urbanization produced slums and pestilence as well as factory unemployment. Growth in government came as a by-product and brought with it a host of problems in public administration and policy-making.[12]

All of this coincided with some fundamental changes in the Supreme Court's interpretation of the Constitution.

"REASONABLE REGULATION"

The perceived maldistribution of income, the problems of urbanization and the deterioration of the environment, and the closing of the frontier contributed significantly to the changing role of government in the late nineteenth century. Since most citizens blamed these problems on imperfections in the market system, not surprisingly they called on government to use its coercive power to alter the results of the market allocation of resources. The initial interpretations of the Constitution clearly encouraged productive activity. But changes in the rules of the game in the late 1800s increased the possibility of nonmarket (noncompensated) transfers and the accompanying resource waste.

Although identifying watersheds in the evolution of these rules is difficult, one Supreme Court case stands out as the beginning of a new era in constitutional interpretation—*Munn* v. *Illinois* (1877), which concerned the power of the Illinois state legislature to set grain storage rates for elevators. As noted earlier, the use of government to affect transfers had existed before 1877. Jonathan R. T. Hughes suggests that the history of the transfer process had its roots in colonial times.[13] Moreover, Harry Scheiber points out that "the road to *Munn*" was a long one, steeped in the tradition of common law.[14] Colonial and even federal precedents for price control cannot be denied, but we should not lose sight of the impact of constitutional limitations on restricting transfers.

Even Hughes, whose main thesis is that nonmarket control has been with us since colonial times and that our history is not the "mother lode of the *laissez faire* tradition," concluded that "we went from mercantilism to neomercantilism with an intervening period, the period from independence to the 1870's when the dominance of the free market as the main method of social control waxed and waned, the period when the private economy continuously moved, by both spread and size effects ahead of government regulatory power."[15]

With the *Munn* decision, however, the door for transfer activity at the federal level was thrown open as the court legitimized governmental regulation of private property. Over time, this process was used increasingly to alter the structure of wealth and power in our society. The *Munn* decision may have been a response to the changing economic and social conditions of the time, but the consequence of the *Munn* doctrine was the encouragement of transfer activity.

The *Munn* case had its roots in agrarian unrest during the post–Civil War period and in the denouncement of monopoly power, rate fixing, and big business in general. This led to the Granger movement and a series of lawsuits known as the *Granger Cases*. In the midwestern states Granger-controlled legislatures had passed laws aimed at regulating the rates of railroads and other "public" utilities. The regulated companies refused to obey the mandates of the regulatory agencies, and numerous cases came before the state supreme courts of Illinois and Wisconsin. Benjamin Twiss characterizes the ensuing battle as Granger individualism versus corporate laissez-faire. "The result," says Twiss, "was not outright laissez faire, nor was it the opposite. Rather was it a compromise which, through the ambiguous guarantee of a 'fair return on the investment,' left the power in the hands of lawyers and judges."[16]

The arguments used by the opposing sides reflect the issues at stake. On the side of regulation were two canons of English common law long used to justify state intervention. The first, *Sic utere tuo ut alienum non laedas* (so use your property as not to injure the property of others), granted police power to the state. Laissez-faireists of the time took this phrase literally and argued that injury required proof of nuisance. But to the Grangers the injury resulted from monopoly power used to exploit farmers through high-priced services. The due process clauses of the Fifth and Fourteenth amendments, however, placed stringent restrictions on police power and forced the backers of regulation to rely upon a second canon. *Salus populi suprema lex* (public welfare is the highest law) justified price regulation for many goods and services in sixteenth-, seventeenth-, and eighteenth-century England and the rising tide of Jacksonian democracy revitalized "public interest" regulation. There was a growing mood in the Supreme Court during Taney's reign to grant state legislatures the power to further the security, morality, and general welfare of the community. The cry for "regulation in the public interest" was increasingly heard in state legislatures.

On the other side of the battle, legal counsel for the railroads and other enterprises affected by the state control of rate setting argued that such laws violated the Fourteenth Amendment and the commerce and contract clauses, as well as the vested rights of property owners. "They first unsuccessfully invoked the obligation of contracts and just compensation clauses, then turned to a claim that unrestricted management was an aspect of the property right. Failing there, they demanded judicial review over legislative and administrative regulation."[17] In a brief filed for the Chicago and Northwestern Railway Company, J. W. Cary asked whether states had the right or power to assume the "management and control" of railroads or any other company. He considered that private property rights included the right to set prices and to bargain freely over the terms of contracts. To an economist writing in *Nation*, "the rights of property exist irrespective of any charter. The right to collect remunerative tolls or fares is not a prerogative right but a natural or common law right."[18] The railroads further argued that "property is chiefly valuable to the owner on account of the income it yields."[19] If "the power to tax was the power to destroy," the power to regulate rail rates surely was the power to destroy the very reason for the existence of companies—the desire to maximize profits. Of course, even the regulators contended that the states should never "reduce the tolls and charges below a standard which will be reasonable or which will afford a fair and adequate remuneration and return upon the amount of capital actually invested."[20] For the opponents of the Granger legislation, however, it was not just the magnitude of rate fixing, but the interference of the states with the enjoyment and use of private property. Said J. W. Cary in his brief, "the rights of the corporators in the property is a vested right that cannot be disturbed by any legislative action, and the right to use, control and fix and charge compensation for its use inheres in the property, and is vested in the corporators, just as absolutely as the right to any property vests in any individual."[21]

The culmination came in 1876 when *Munn* v. *Illinois* was argued before the U.S. Supreme Court. In the lower courts counsel for the plaintiff had argued in terms of the taking of private property: "For the first time since the union of the states a legislature of a state has attempted to control the property, capital and labor of a private individual by fixing the prices he may receive from other private persons who choose to deal with him."[22] One of the lawyers for the railroad, W. C. Goudy, argued that the Illinois legislation fixing storage rates for grain warehouses was "a bald attempt to disable those engaged in the commerce of the country from making their own contract, and to prevent prices from being regulated by the general commercial laws of the country."[23] Benjamin Twiss describes the legislation as a "naked attempt to take property from the owner and give it to another person when it was not necessary for the public use, and without compensation."[24] With this act the state of Illinois clearly allowed transfer activity. The only remaining question was the action of the Supreme Court.

For many there was little doubt that the Supreme Court would overturn lower court decisions on the *Granger Cases* and eliminate the possibility of transfers through regulation. The panic of 1873 had changed the ownership and structure of railroads. Said one Chicago newspaper, "Railroads have become an article of merchandise, sold regularly at auction, not by capital stock but according to value, including a preferred portion of debt. The expenses of running railroads have been reduced; dividends are fewer and smaller. Retrenchment has become essential to life . . . The rates have so fallen that the popular complaint which led to State legislation no longer exists."[25] An article in the 1875 volume of the *American Law Review* captured the feeling of many members of the bar:

> The late war left the average American politician with a powerful desire to acquire property from other people without paying for it. A succession of schemes, too familiar to recapitulate here, have been tried, and, after hard struggles, have been defeated by the honest common sense of the community. We have sufficient faith in the speedy clarification of ideas, among the honest advocates of the so-called Granger laws, to feel confident that this assault upon private property will soon lose their support . . . When that decision is reached, we believe it will then be received with general favor throughout the whole country. It is necessary in order to restore public confidence in the rights of private property, now severely shaken.[26]

The court's March 1, 1877, decision on *Munn* and other *Granger Cases* surprised those who were sure that such regulation would be found unconstitutional. Chief Justice Morrison Waite spoke for the majority and revolutionized regulation law:

> Property does become clothed with a public interest when used in a manner to make it of public consequence, and affect the community at large. When, therefore, one devotes his property to a use in which the public has an interest, he, in effect, grants to the public an interest in that use, and must submit to be controlled by the public for the common good, to the extent of the interest he has thus created.[27]

Under the doctrine of police power, the Supreme Court had previously upheld the power of the states to regulate economic activity incidentally. But the idea that private property used in the public interest was subject to public regulation gave a broad new authority to the government to interfere with contracts and private property.[28] Such authority raised the returns to transfer activity by giving non-owners the potential to affect resource allocation. Associate Justice Stephen Field, recognizing the path-breaking nature of this decision, said in his dissent, "If this be sound law, if there be no protection, either in the principles upon which our republican government is founded, or in the prohibitions of the Constitution against such invasion of private rights, all property and all business in the State are held at the mercy of a majority of its legislature."[29] To Field the constitutional protection of life, liberty, and property extended "to the use and income of property, as well as to its title and possession."[30] His broad interpretation in *Munn* v. *Illinois* of property and liberty was similar to his expression in the *Slaughterhouse Cases*. "Liberty," said Field, "means freedom to go where one may choose, and to act in such a manner not inconsistent with the equal rights of others, as his judgment may dictate for the promotion of his happiness; that is, to pursue such callings and avocations as may be most suitable to develop his capacities, and give to them their highest enjoyment."[31] Dissenting in *Stone* v. *Wisconsin* (1877), he continued to decry the *Munn* decision by saying that it "will justify the legislature in fixing the price of all articles, and the compensation for all services. It sanctions intermeddling with all business and pursuits and property in the community, leaving the use and enjoyment of property and the compensation for its use to the discretion of the legislature."[32] Fifteen years later, Justice David J. Brewer reiterated Field's dissent:

> The paternal theory of government is to me odious. The utmost possible liberty to the individual, and the fullest possible protection to him and his property, is both the limitation and the duty of government. If it may

regulate the price of one service, which is not a public service, or the compensation for the use of one kind of property which is not devoted to a public use, why may it not with equal degree regulate the price of all service and the compensation to be paid for the use of all property?[33]

The implications of the *Munn* decision were obvious to others besides the dissenting Supreme Court justices. To the *St. Paul Pioneer Press*, for example, "the decision places the corporations at the mercy of the Legislatures, deprives the capital invested in railroads of all security, and by transferring the control of their property interests from the corporation to the State Legislature, renders it liable to be at any time confiscated by ignorant, capricious or vindictive legislation."[34] Similarly, the *New York Times* wrote "that if each State may decide for itself what rates are reasonable, the holders of railroad stocks and bonds can have no guarantee against the application of a measure which might practically amount to confiscation . . . and great properties may be placed at the mercy of a power which is essentially capricious."[35] But perhaps the best insight into the effect of the Granger laws came from William C. Goudy in his brief before the Illinois Supreme Court:

If a majority of one legislature can fix prices for the minority, so in turn that minority can obtain power at another legislature and fix prices for the products or merchandise of their adversaries. When capital is in control the price will be fixed; when labor holds the power the investment of the capitalists must suffer. The price of corn may be made high today, and reduced tomorrow. All trade and commerce will be destroyed, and a struggle at the polls will be the substitute for natural laws of supply and demand.[36]

Although *Munn* v. *Illinois* made large-scale transfers possible, its full impact was not felt for several decades. A major reason for the delay in transfer activity was the rise of "substantive due process," believed by some to be the bulwark of laissez-faireism in the late nineteenth century.[37] In 1868 the Fourteenth Amendment was passed in an effort to clarify the rights of the newly freed slaves. A part of the amendment read: "No State shall . . . deprive any person of life, liberty or property, without due process of law." This, of course, was similar to the Fifth Amendment, which put the same sort of limitations on federal laws but was simply a procedural safeguard guaranteeing just compensation. Before the Civil War, due process required that certain procedures be fulfilled before a person could be deprived of life, liberty, or property.

But supporters of the Fourteenth Amendment hoped that it would give more substance to due process.

Interpretation of the Fourteenth Amendment during the last quarter of the century introduced the concept of substance into due process, but the extent to which this guaranteed private property against arbitrary or confiscatory laws is not clear. The earliest interpretations diverged little from the procedural notion of due process seen in the *Slaughterhouse Cases* of 1873. There the Supreme Court had decided that Louisiana's grant of monopoly rights to the slaughterhouse trade in New Orleans did not violate due process. However, in *Davidson* v. *New Orleans* (1878), vested rights gained added substance as the majority of the court argued that a law transferring private property from individual A to individual B would in fact violate due process *even* if the transfer followed established procedures. The words of Justice Samuel Miller in this opinion sounded much like those of Marshall during the early national period, but the ruling's impact on vested rights was short-lived. In *Stone* v. *Farmers' Loan and Trust Co.* (1886), another rail regulation case, the court re-emphasized the *Munn* doctrine but added the opinion—with the implication that this addition would provide substance—that regulation was not without limits. Four years later in *Chicago, Milwaukee and St. Paul Railroad Co.* v. *Minnesota*, the doctrine of substantive due process was expanded when the court held that state regulation must be reasonable. The definition of reasonableness, however, was left to the independent judiciary.

Although this interpretation of substantive due process provided constitutional protection against "unreasonable" transfers of property, the question of reasonableness left great scope to the judicial review process. Could vested rights be ensured in such a situation?

> The question of the reasonableness or arbitrariness of a law could not be settled by reference to any specific constitutional provision or any absolute principle of law. A reasonable law was one that seemed sensible, plausible, and intelligent to the judges who passed upon it. What constituted sensible, plausible, and intelligent public policy, however, is largely a matter of the individual's economic and social philosophy—his standard of values. When the Court applied the test of reasonableness to legislation, therefore, it measured the law against its own economic and social attitudes. If in the light of these attitudes the law seemed intelligent, the justices upheld it; if not, they declared it unreasonable, arbitrary, and a violation of due process of law.[38]

The due process clause clearly offered little or no firm protection against transfers and was subject to the predilections of the justices. It is therefore not surprising that the definition of reasonable changed over time, depending on the economic and social pressures of the moment. In 1898, a Supreme Court decision held that regulating the hours of miners was reasonable under state police power; but in a similar case in 1905 the court ruled that regulating the hours in bakeshops was unreasonable.[39]

The lack of firm constitutional arguments and the relevance of nonconstitutional information became even clearer in *Muller* v. *Oregon* (1908). In this case, the constitutionality of a 1903 Oregon statute regulating the working hours of women was at issue. Oregon retained Louis Brandeis to argue its side. In support of the "reasonableness" of the statute Brandeis filed a brief consisting of only two pages dealing with constitutional arguments and over a hundred pages dealing with social conditions. Since reasonableness was the issue, he argued that evidence was needed on that question rather than on the constitutionality question.

With the acceptance by the court of the Brandeis brief, the rule of "higher law" lost much of its power. This in turn raised the benefits of using the judicial and legislative processes to acquire command over resources. Cases involving regulation of working hours, working conditions, and prices became more numerous on court dockets. Regulatory agencies began to evolve and gain power to influence resource allocation. For example, the Interstate Commerce Commission, the first of numerous federal regulatory bodies, was created in 1887. Since this regulatory power provided numerous opportunities to use the coercive power of government to influence the allocation of resources and the distribution of income, the benefits from transfer activity increased significantly.

Other traditional governmental functions were also altered during this period in ways that made transfer activity more profitable. First, government's power to tax was expanded. As late as 1875, the Supreme Court held that a state law authorizing the use of tax monies for the encouragement of private businesses was unconstitutional.[40] However, by the beginning of the next century, taxes were recognized as an accepted method of regulating market outcomes. In *McCray* v. *United States* (1904), for example, the court upheld a statute that regulated margarine production by placing a tax of ten cents per pound on artificially colored margarine but only one-fourth cent per pound on the uncolored product. The approval of this tax opened a new arena for potential transfer activity and effectively removed the limits on Congress's power to use taxes for nonrevenue purposes. The Sixteenth Amendment (1913) authorized the income tax and further strengthened the hands of those who wished to use the coercive powers of government in their favor.

Second, between 1875 and 1920 the police power of the state was increasingly used to justify interference with contracts and the power to regulate interstate commerce to justify federal intervention in the market. In *Champion* v. *Ames* (1903), under the guise of controlling interstate commerce, the court upheld a law forbidding the shipment of lottery tickets. Two years later, in *Swift and Co.* v. *United States*, the court formulated the "stream of commerce" doctrine, which holds that economic activities that might eventually be part of interstate commerce are subject to federal control. This doctrine has expanded until now almost all production and distribution is subject to such control because of its potential involvement in interstate commerce.

Third, in series of cases between 1892 and 1911 the court substantially expanded the power of the legislative branch to grant discretionary power to the executive.[41] Congress had only to outline the basic policy objectives; a regulatory board or commission could then implement the mechanics of the law, writing rules as it saw fit. This culminated in *United States* v. *Grimaud* (1911) in which the court decreed that administrative rulings had the force of law. The implications of executive lawmaking for transfer activity were tremendous. No longer did those desiring laws written to favor a special interest group have to convince an entire legislature—only the members of a small regulatory board. With this, the "tyranny of the minority" was added to the "tyranny of the majority" so feared by Madison.

These changes in the institutional environment increased transfer activity. It has been said that the history of lobbying is the history of legislation; but after 1880 the level of these efforts, especially by industry and railroads, rose to an unprecedented amount. In addition to illegal expenditures on bribery, company attorneys ran for public offices, corporations contributed to campaign funds, and favors were given to elected officials. A market in state legislative seats developed, and even the outcomes of gubernatorial and congressional races depended on the ability of companies to buy votes.[42] With the rise of substantive due process and the rule of reasonableness, efforts to influence court decisions commanded much attention. The power of business during this period is demonstrated by the emasculation of the *Munn* doctrine. During the Republican reign from 1868 to 1912, the court system—from the Supreme Court to lower federal and state judiciaries—was filled with corporate lawyers sympathetic to the interests of big business.[43] With the quasi-legislative power obtained by the courts during this era, the independent judiciary was in a position to determine not just the constitutionality of acts but also the reasonableness of a transfer of rights from one individual or group to another. With this concentration of power, it is little wonder that resources were invested to obtain and prevent such transfers.

Between the periods of colonial government intervention under the guise of mercantilism and the changes that occurred during the last quarter of the nineteenth century, America's experiment with constitutional government was at least a partial success. Liberty and property rights were protected by both the Constitution and its judicial interpretation. The effect was to encourage productivity and discourage transfers. By 1915, however, the major barriers erected by the Founding Fathers against large-scale legislative transfers had been dramatically lessened or removed altogether. The general reverence for natural (vested) rights had diminished (the Supreme Court last used it in 1875). The contract clause, formerly a bulwark against transfer activity, was greatly weakened by the bankruptcy case of 1827. The commerce clause had changed from a limit on state action into a justification for federal action. The due process clause, which had been viewed as a revival of vested rights in the move from procedural to substantive due process, had been rendered ineffective because of the ambiguity of the rule of reasonableness. All of this, coupled with changes in the constitutional interpretation of the public interest in *Munn* v. *Illinois* meant that the groundwork had been laid for the birth of a transfer society.

EIGHT
←——————→

Nothing New:
World War I to Present

The transfer society established by 1917 has grown in the last sixty years, but its essential character has not changed. More recent Supreme Court rulings conform to the views expressed in *Munn* and other decisions. Both at home and abroad, the growth of the transfer society has led to the growth of government—a phenomenon that concerns many.

To students of Karl Marx, Joseph Schumpeter, Friedrich Hayek, or even Adam Smith, the increase in governmental control of the economy should come as no surprise. Explanations of when, why, and to what extent the government has made inroads into the private property structure often conflict, however. An examination of any twentieth-century American history book provides a long list of starting points and possible explanations for the rise of government. The income tax amendment, World War I, the Great Depression, the New Deal, World War II, and the Fair Deal, to mention a few, suggest that the crises of this century must be included in any explanation. John Kenneth Galbraith contends that big government must countervail big business and big labor, which have gained so much power in the twentieth century. Arthur Schlesinger, Jr., has argued that the cold war and the ensuing arms race account for our Leviathan.[1]

Jonathan R. T. Hughes, on the other hand, suggests that the "governmental habit" of growing antedates 1900.[2] Hughes seems to recognize, more than many authors describing the twentieth century, that the past seventy years have witnessed little that is new in our institutional structure. In introducing a section entitled "Progressives and the Impact of World War I," he states:

> Indeed, if this book were merely a descriptive history, this section, which treats the First World War from our perspective, would be a separate episode. But in certain crucial respects the development of our social control structure in 1917 and 1918 was a continuation of the changes wrought by the agrarian radicals, the Populists, and their successors in the Progressive movement.[3]

But even Hughes cannot resist the temptation of focusing on characteristics unique to this century and of arguing that without these, the transfer society would not have been possible: "The point we want to emphasize here is that the wars of our century made such expansions of federal power possible."[4] The events that disrupted normal economic life in the 1900s have affected our institutional structure and the Constitution. But the changes since 1917 that have further encouraged transfer activity reflect the principle of regulation in the public interest, expansion of pricing and taxing power, the rule of reasonableness, and the stream of commerce doctrine promulgated between 1877 and 1917.

NOTHING NEW FROM THE COURT

President Woodrow Wilson was a major architect of governmental reform and his efforts from 1913 to 1917 were at least partially responsible for changes in constitutional interpretation that furthered the transfer society. However, the entry of the United States into World War I halted the reform movement and marked the end of the most significant era of constitutional change in U.S. history. From 1877 to 1917 the Constitution was altered in numerous ways that made transfers much easier to obtain. Except for the income tax amendment, all of these changes came through interpretation. Although the full fruits of these changes were not seen for several decades, the constitutional basis for a transfer society had been laid.

A few events in the period from 1917 to the present, one of which was World War I itself, increased the growth of transfers. During that war, President Wilson requested and received emergency executive powers enabling him to implement programs far beyond the ordinary scope of government. Commodity prices could be fixed, plants nationalized, and the distribution of food licensed and regulated. The emergency powers conferred on the executive branch in World War I clearly offered many opportunities for transfers since they represented considerable attenuation of property rights. Although not all of these powers were used, their establishment did set the stage for later arguments that extraordinary conditions required extraordinary intervention by the government and that the Constitution could be effectively ignored during such times. Since the meaning of "extraordinary" was debatable, the introduction of these war powers opened another area where resources could be (and were) invested to obtain and to prevent transfers.

With the end of the war and the advent of the Roaring Twenties, the Supreme Court withdrew from its previous interventionist position in economic affairs and returned to a more laissez faire doctrine. The amorphousness of the rule of reasonableness under substantive due process eased this transition. No new constitutional ground had to be broken; the justices had only to find the regulations in question unreasonable. A case in point was *Adkins* v. *Children's Hospital* (1923), which involved the constitutionality of a District of Columbia minimum wage law. The court declared the law unconstitutional under due process even though previous court decisions had upheld laws regulating hours worked per day. The distinction between interfering with the freedom to contract for the length of the workday and the freedom to contract for wages is difficult to make on objective grounds. But the rule of reasonableness allowed the court enough flexibility to make this subjective distinction. The initial return to a freedom of contract doctrine involved transfer activity, but for the ensuing decade it also made transfers more difficult to obtain.

Another ambiguous doctrine used by the court during the 1920s to promote a laissez faire economic policy was that of "the public interest." Recall that *Munn* v. *Illinois* in 1877 formalized the idea that any business affected with the public interest was subject to public regulation. In the forty years following *Munn* this doctrine was used primarily to further government alteration of property rights. However, from 1920 to 1930 the court adamantly declared that the actions of most businesses did not affect the public interest and thus were not subject to regulation.[5] This declaration did weaken government but offered no firm long-run protection against transfers. The substitution of an equivocal concept like public interest for firm constitutional limitations meant that the subjective judgment of justices was supreme.

Probably the most famous economic event in U.S. history is the Great Depression. It is seen as a watershed in almost every type of economic activity—most significantly, the relation between the public and the private sectors. Although we recognize the cataclysmic nature of economic conditions in the 1930s, we do not see this period as one that introduced dramatically new constitutional interpretations that promoted transfer activity. True, the economic crisis stimulated a great outcry for governmental action and such action was forthcoming, but no new constitutional ground was needed to justify the government's large-scale economic intervention. The interpretations of the Constitution from 1877 to 1917 provided ample precedent for most New Deal programs.

Franklin Roosevelt acted quickly on his mandate in the 1932 election. The Emergency Banking Act, requiring the surrender of all gold and gold certificates to the Treasury Department, became law on March 9, 1933. In addition a Joint Congressional Resolution in June of that year nullified the gold clause in all private contracts. Since certain contracts specified payment in gold (by weight), this law and resolution represented a clear challenge to the constitutional protection of freedom of contract. Other restrictions on voluntary trade and individual decisions followed. The Agricultural Adjustment Act in May 1933 expanded the power of government to restrict production of several agricultural commodities in return for federal payments. The National Industrial Recovery Act provided for cartelization of much of American industry through industrial groups that would draft codes of fair competition carrying the force of law. The Tennessee Valley Authority, created in 1933, was given the authority to engage in the production of electrical power and fertilizer. Various other programs transferred control of much agricultural and forest land from the private to the public sector. These programs and numerous others represented an effort by Roosevelt and the New Deal Congress to alleviate the economic crisis.

The courts' view of the New Deal program, however, was not clear. The relation between production and interstate commerce, the theory of emergency powers, and the provision for the general welfare were offered as constitutional justifications for the legislative enactments. In opposition were the doctrines of due process, separation of powers, states' rights, and the public interest, which could be used to negate the statutes. Supreme Court approval of the New Deal package depended largely on whether it followed the broad constitutional interpretations of the 1877–1917 period or the decisions of the 1920s.

Judges sympathizing with the New Deal social objectives and appreciating the liberal national tradition would find it easy to select a stream of precedents validating most of the New Deal measures. On the other hand, judges who sympathized with the conservative crescendo of protest against the New Deal's interference with private property rights and who accepted the traditions of *laissez-faire* economics and limited federal power would have little difficulty in finding justification for striking down as unconstitutional most of the important New Deal statutes.[6]

The justices chose the latter course. The court's review of New Deal statutes began in 1935, and in the next sixteen months ten major cases were decided. In eight of the ten the court decided against the government, negating a significant portion of the legislative recovery program.[7] The Agricultural Adjustment Act, the National Industrial Recovery Act, and several other important laws were declared unconstitutional. Only the monetary program, including Congress's right to negate the gold clause in contracts, and the Tennessee Valley Authority were upheld by the court. The court's sanctioning of the monetary programs did indicate how powerless the contract clause had become. It held that the government clearly had the right to abrogate private contracts that prevented the rightful exercise of federal functions. Since the federal government was constitutionally responsible for establishing and maintaining the monetary system, it could, with a stroke of a pen, nullify all clauses in contracts specifying payment in a certain form, in this case gold.

Roosevelt won re-election in 1936 and immediately set about reducing the court's power to nullify his program. Judicial reform had been a major issue in the election campaign, with numerous proposals for limiting judicial power forthcoming. An amendment was even proposed to deny the court the power to declare any act of Congress unconstitutional. Other amendments would have required approval of two-thirds of the court to declare congressional acts unconstitutional or allowed a two-thirds vote in both houses of Congress to overturn a judicial "veto." Roosevelt's proposal was not as dramatic and did not require a constitutional amendment. He simply suggested that membership of the Supreme Court be expanded to fifteen. The court-packing scheme split the Democratic majority in Congress and was eventually defeated. However, the issue became moot in 1937 when the court began approving New Deal legislation. In a remarkable turnaround, the justices found constitutional precedent for almost all of the legislation brought before them. Again, these were not path-breaking decisions because ample precedent was available from the interventionist period before World War I. Transfers were allowed and did become more prevalent, but without new constitutional doctrines to justify them.

Only two cases, *Nebbia* v. *New York* (1934), and *N.L.R.B.* v. *Jones and Laughlin Steel Corporation* (1937), were of substantial importance to the economy, and both simply expanded on previously existing doctrines. In *Nebbia* v. *New York* the court upheld a New York law giving a state milk control board the power to set maximum and minimum prices for milk. The court justified its action under the public interest doctrine first set forth in *Munn* v. *Illinois* and in the process removed any lingering ambiguity as to when economic activity was "affected with a public interest." It held that all activity was so defined and that a state could adopt "whatever economic policy may reasonably be deemed to promote public welfare."[8] Previously the *Munn* doctrine had promoted significant transfer activity. Now it was even clearer that the government had favors to hand out and privileges to withhold.

The *N.L.R.B.* case also served to clarify and strengthen a previously established arena of transfer activity. In *Swift and Co.* v. *United States* (1905), the Court had formulated the stream of commerce doctrine that was subsequently used many times to justify different government enactments. However, its application was somewhat restricted since it applied only to transportation and distribution of commodities. Thus part of the economic processes, particularly the direct production of commodities, was not subject to regulation under the commerce clause. In *N.L.R.B.* v. *Jones and Laughlin Steel Corporation* the court expanded the stream of commerce doctrine to include all production, arguing that the materials for the production process *likely* were drawn from interstate commerce and *likely* went back into interstate commerce. Thus after 1937 the commerce clause of the Constitution became a springboard for much legislation. It was no longer necessary to show that the economic actors being regulated were an immediate part of the stream of commerce or that the volume of business was so large as to ensure that interstate commerce was involved. All economic activity was potentially involved in interstate commerce and hence subject to federal regulation.

In a series of cases following *N.L.R.B.* v. *Jones and Laughlin Steel Corporation*, the court made it clear that the stream of commerce doctrine applied to all production of goods and services. Small businesses shipping across state lines, farmers selling in national markets, power companies selling all of their output within a single state were all subject to federal regulation under the commerce clause. The first federal minimum wage law was also upheld because of the relation between most employment and interstate commerce. The commerce clause, originally seen as a firm barrier against interference in economic activity by individual states, became a justification for federal control of nearly all such activity.

Along with the rise of regulation under the commerce clause, the 1940s saw the due process clause of the Fourteenth Amendment reinstated as a foundation for the rule of reasonableness. From 1937 to 1947 only one state statute was declared unconstitutional by the Supreme Court because it was contrary to the due process clause.[9]

World War II brought much the same threat to constitutional government as did World War I, and the precedents for interference in the economy were followed quite closely. Again, significant new constitutional doctrines did not have to be forged, but the war did lead to a substantial increase in the role of government.

We lack enough perspective to evaluate court decisions since the close of World War II, but the main thrust of the period seems to have been the expansion and codification of the constitutional alterations of the 1877–1917 period. Interpretation of the taxing power, the police power, the commerce clause, and due process and equal protection under the Fourteenth Amendment in ways that encourage coercive transfers of rights has continued. The court has quite clearly been an activist one, but it has used previously established doctrines to build our transfer society.

EVIDENCE OF THE TRANSFER SOCIETY

Thus far we have argued that the institutional changes increasing the return to transfer activity relative to productive activity have fostered negative-sum games. A consistent data series documenting this transition would be useful. Unfortunately, however, quantifying transfer and productive activities is difficult because the two are not easily separable. Perhaps one of the better ways of illustrating this point is to consider the standard measure of economic growth, gross national product (GNP). One might predict from our analysis that the birth and growth of a transfer society should reduce economic growth. Yet growth statistics from the Civil War to the present do not substantiate this. To the contrary, the growth in real output per capita, as shown in Table 1, averaged nearly 1.8 percent between 1860 and 1970—an impressive rate by any standard. Moreover, only during the period that includes the Great Depression do the growth estimates deviate from their upward march. Even then real growth is greater than 1 percent.

There are, however, two problems with inferring from these data that the transfer society does not reduce real economic growth. First, there is reason to suspect that GNP statistics do not reflect negative-sum transfer activity. Should we expect the GNP to decline with increasing amounts of transfer activity? Since the GNP is the value of final goods and *services*, the answer is no. If a lobbyist is hired and sent to Washington to obtain favors from government, the services of the lobbyist are added into the GNP. If a lawyer or accountant is hired to obtain or prevent transfers of rights, his services are added to measures of real output. Furthermore, if the productivity of the individuals performing such services increases (that is, if per unit of effort more transfers can be affected or more prevented), measured GNP per capita rises. The point therefore is that the behavior of the GNP is not a good indicator of the extent of positive-sum games. Separating the services of an accountant hired to improve a firm's efficiency from those of one hired to encourage a regulatory commission to regulate rates in a monopoly fashion is difficult, to say the least. Both types of services will enter positively into output measures, but each will have different effects on the total wealth of the society. Standard measures of per capita income therefore do not capture the

TABLE 1

PER CAPITA CHANGES IN REAL OUTPUT
UNITED STATES
(percentage)

1860–1880	1.28[a]
1880–1900	1.38
1900–1920	1.63
1920–1940	1.15
1940–1960	2.18
1950–1970	2.23
1960–1970	2.62

SOURCE: U.S., Bureau of the Census, *Historical Statistics of the United States, Colonial Times to 1970,* Bicentennial ed., part 1 (Washington, D.C.: Government Printing Office, 1975), p. 254.

[a]Rates are average annual rates for each twenty-year time period.

negative-sum aspects of transfer activity, necessitating a look at other evidence of our entry into the transfer society.

The second problem with twentieth-century growth data is that our transfer society may be so young that the results of reduced productive activity have not yet manifested themselves. To see the effects of long-term transfer activity, it is useful to examine what Samuel Brittan has referred to as the "British sickness."[10] The data shown in Table 2 demonstrate the lag in British growth compared with other advanced countries. Estimates suggest "that the average level of output per head in sixteen industrial countries rose sixfold between 1870 and 1976, but only fourfold in the United Kingdom."[11] Brittan offers several explanations for these growth rates, including government spending, tax perversities, the class system, and union power, but his section on democracy and interest groups is most pertinent to our analysis. After quoting extensively from Henry Simons (who "raises the question of the effects of uncertain property rights on investment")[12] Brittan concludes that

a system of confused and unpredictable property rights under a nominally private enterprise system is highly discouraging to investment—and there-

TABLE 2

LONG-TERM GROWTH RATES
REAL GROSS DOMESTIC PRODUCT (GDP) PER CAPITA
(1970 U.S. dollars)

	Average of 16 Advanced Countries[a]	United Kingdom
Annual growth (percentage)		
1870–1976	1.8	1.3
1870–1913	1.5	1.0
1913–1950	1.1	1.0
1950–1970	3.8	2.3
1970–1976	2.4	2.0
GDP per capita in U.S. 1970 dollars		
1870	$ 666	$ 956
1976	$4,258	$3,583
Ratio of U.K. to average GDP per capita		
1870		1.44
1976		0.84

SOURCE: Based on Samuel Brittan, "How British Is the British Sickness?" *Journal of Law and Economics* 21, no. 2 (October 1978):246.

[a]Arithmetical average of United States, Canada, Australia, Japan, United Kingdom, Germany, France, Italy, Switzerland, Netherlands, Belgium, Sweden, Denmark, Norway, Austria, Finland.

by also depressing to employment in the longer run . . . Collective action
to secure real wages incompatible with full employment may come not
just through the strike threat alone, but also through political action—
import price ceilings, minimum wage laws, and farm support are only
some of the more obvious areas. The uncertainty and insecurity of
property rights which Simons feared can be the result of regulatory
agencies or of congressional hyperactivity as well as of unions. The real
danger is that the end result of action taken by people through collective
activity will be unacceptable to the same people in their capacity of consumers and voters—a perverse invisible hand. *The fact that Simons was pre-
mature in his forebodings in the case of the United States does not mean that they
can be dismissed.* (emphasis added)[13]

This final sentence answers the question that Brittan poses in the title of
his paper, "How British is the British Sickness?" Although the growth
rate in the United States has not lagged as much as that of the United
Kingdom, it would be unsafe to conclude that we are not a transfer
society.

The United Kingdom is not the only example of the impact of
transfer activity on economic growth. Anne O. Krueger's seminal article,
"The Political Economy of the Rent-Seeking Society," concludes that
7.3 percent—not an insignificant amount—of India's national income
was devoted to the type of transfer activity we have been describing. In
Turkey the returns to import licenses alone amounted to 15 percent of
GNP in 1968.[14] And in Sweden there are indications that transfer activity
is taking its toll on positive-sum activities. Today the public sector in
Sweden controls 64 percent of GNP, up from 24 percent in 1950. In
order to finance the many transfer programs of the welfare state, taxes
have risen dramatically. It has been estimated that "if the married
breadwinner (wife not working) with four children earned $4,600 per
year in 1978, the net income (after taxes are subtracted and transfers are
added) would be $14,117. The family also earns $14,117 when the
breadwinner's gross income is $23,000. Thus, increasing one's salary
from $4,600 to $23,000 has absolutely no effect on the family's *net*
income position."[15] Between 1960 and 1978 this perverse system of
taxation has resulted in a 24 percent decline in work time, a 70 percent
decrease in overtime, and a 63 percent increase in absenteeism. Guesses
are that 10 percent of Sweden's GNP goes unrecorded as a result of
black-market and barter activity.[16] Estimates of this "irregular economy"
in the United States range from 10 to 26 percent of the total economy.[17]

Again these figures do not provide a precise estimate of the effect of transfer activity on real output, but they do indicate its direction and give some idea of its magnitude.

With this background as a basis for comparison, let us turn to the U.S. experience. One of the obvious proxies for growth in transfer activity is growth in government, although it should be re-emphasized that governmental efforts include an element of productive activity and that transfer activity occurs in the private sector. Allan Meltzer and Scott Richard conclude from the data on the growth of taxes, employment, and income that "even in the United States, with a long history of coexistence between market freedom and political freedom, state intervention in the market has grown, and the size of government has grown. Growth of government is not a simple transfer of power from one group to another. Well-functioning markets disperse power; growth of government concentrates power."[18] Columns 2 and 4 of Table 3 show that government has grown approximately 60 to 200 percent faster than the private sector whether measured by total taxes relative to real GNP or by government employment relative to total employment. In attempting to explain this growth, Meltzer and Richard dismiss the idea that it was caused by "a few chance events" and observe that

> as more business is done with the state, relationships develop between government agencies and corporations. Within the business sector, groups develop that see their interests joined to those of the political bureaucracy. Although businessmen may for a time retain the rhetoric of hostility to

TABLE 3

COMPOUND ANNUAL RATES OF GROWTH OF GOVERNMENT

	1	*2*	*3*	*4*
Period	Total Taxes (1978 dollars) (percentage)	Taxes/Real GNP[a]	Total Government Employment (percentage)	Government Employment/ Total Employment[b]
1901–1974	8.08	2.55	3.46	2.14
1901–1929	7.29	2.28	3.43	1.67
1929–1951	9.59	3.28	3.40	2.70
1951–1974	7.58	2.25	3.56	2.27

SOURCE: Calculated from data in Allan H. Meltzer and Scott F. Richard, "Why Government Grows (and Grows) in a Democracy," *Public Interest* no. 52 (Summer, 1978): 112.

[a]The ratio of the growth rate in taxes to the growth rate in real GNP.

[b]The ratio of the growth rate in total government employment to the growth rate in total employment.

"government," a growing number find reason to support the expansion of agencies and programs relevant to their interests.[19]

There is no better description of a transfer society unless it would be one that added that corporations are not the only bedfellows of government agencies.

INTEREST GROUPS AND TRANSFER ACTIVITY

To illustrate this symbiotic relation between government and private interests and to demonstrate the extent of transfer activity since *Munn* v. *Illinois*, we turn to examples of groups attempting to obtain or prevent transfers. If the United States gave birth to a transfer society during the last quarter of the nineteenth century and if that society has continued to grow, we would expect to see increasing resources devoted to transfer activity. One method of employing these resources is through interest groups and organizations, which have gained increasing support since the Civil War.

> Organization in the last half of the 19th century was more than a matter of clubs and societies. Noticeably, many strong interest groups developed— labor unions, industrial combines, farmers' organizations, occupational associations—to jockey for position and power in society. These groups molded, dominated, shaped American law.
>
> A group or association has two aspects: it defines some persons in, and some persons out. People joined together in groups not simply for mutual help, but to exclude, to define an enemy, to make common cause against outsiders. Organization was a law of life, not merely because life was so complicated, but also because life seemed so much a zero-sum game.[20]

The transfers these groups effected were zero sum since they took from one group and gave to another, but this taking and giving was not self-generated. The groups were organized to effect or prevent transfers, depending on whether they were giving or receiving. "Men and women joined in large, staffed and disciplined program groups such as our public life had not seen before."[21] Examples of this organizational activity include the Grange (founded 1867), the Farmers' Alliance (1874 and 1887), the Knights of Labor (1869), the American Federation of Labor (1881), the American Woman Suffrage Association and the

National Woman Suffrage Association (1869), the United States Brewers Association (1862), the National Potters Association (1886), and the National Association of Manufacturers (1895).

Of all these groups, perhaps none were more influential than the farm groups responsible for the Granger laws that eventually led to the *Munn* decision in 1877. Of course, not all of these organizations and not all of their efforts were aimed at transfer activity, but a significant proportion of their efforts was directed at changing the rules of the game. Aggregate estimates of membership in farm organizations over time do not exist, but Figure 1 shows the growth of three of the major groups, the National Grange, the Farmers Union, and the Farm Bureau. Given the relative stability of rural population during this time and the decline in farm employment, an increasing portion of the agricultural population was organized. We recognize that not all activities of farm organizations were transfer oriented, but there is good reason to believe that membership figures indicate at least the direction of transfer activity. The "Grange Guide Posts" set up in 1942 stated that "the prime purpose of

FIGURE 1
FARM ORGANIZATION MEMBERSHIP
(thousands)

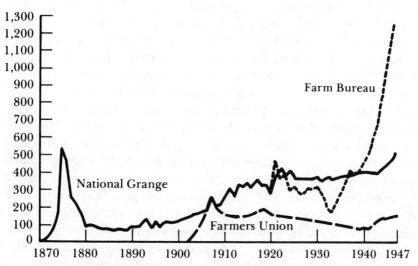

SOURCE: Based on Orville Merton Kile, *The Farm Bureau Through Three Decades* (Baltimore: Waverly Press, 1948), p. 368.

NOTE: Grange membership is divided by 1.6 (Grange's estimate) to place it on a family basis comparable to the Union and the Bureau.

government is to protect its citizens from aggression—both physical and *economic* [emphasis added]."[22] A careful study of the efforts of the Grange in the area of legislation led one student of the group's activities to conclude that "it is universally conceded by those familiar with the facts that one of the great contributions the Grange has made to the American Way of Life is its part in promoting the interests of Agriculture within the halls of legislation; in defending the welfare of the rural people; and in supporting the cause of good government."[23] During its early years most Grange efforts were at the state and local levels; the results are evidenced by the *Munn* decision. But by 1918 attention was turning to Washington. In that year the annual meeting resolved that "the sum of $10,000, or so much thereof as may be necessary, is hereby appropriated for the maintenance of said Washington headquarters; all bills to be approved and paid as other bills against the National Grange are paid."[24] By 1943 the Washington effort was being run from a building purchased for $300,000 and paid for by local chapters.

The activities of the farm groups were justified by their relationship to general welfare. It has been argued that the Grange "has always kept in mind the general public welfare and has never swerved from that policy to the extent of seeking special favors for agriculture—simply a square deal and genuine equality of opportunity for the food producers of the land."[25] The farmers' share of national income was below what was considered "fair"; prices dictated by the markets were "too low" relative to farmers' expectations. In the eyes of a farmer a portion of the true social value of his product was not accruing to the rightful owner; somewhere in the market system property rights had been attenuated, and he called on the government to correct the situation. The success of the farmers' effort is evident in the farm policy of the federal government during this century. Acts such as the Cooperative Marketing Bill of 1922, which exempted co-ops from antitrust legislation, the McNary-Haugen bill of 1924 which would have enabled government purchases of surplus commodities, and the New Deal price-support programs exemplify the success of organizations engaged in transfer activity. "By the end of the 1930's the agricultural price-support program, the basic program desired by the farmer, had become institutionalized into the American political structure, and has continued so in one form or another since that time."[26]

Another indication of the extent of transfer activity is found in the growth of trade associations after the Civil War. Figure 2 shows that

FIGURE 2
NUMBER OF TRADE ASSOCIATIONS
ORGANIZED PER PERIOD,
1860–1938

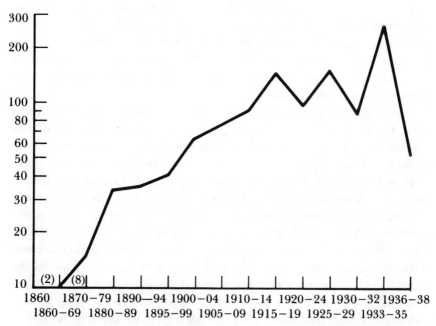

SOURCE: Based on Temporary National Economic Committee, *Trade Association Survey*, prepared by Charles Albert Pearce, Monograph no. 18 (Washington, D.C.: Government Printing Office, 1941), p. 369.

association activity began about the time that we argue the transfer society began in the United States. Of the 1,167 trade associations in existence in 1938, only 2 were founded before 1860. Furthermore, except for the early 1930s when trade organizations were encouraged by the National Recovery Administration, the largest percentage increase in associations came between the 1870s and 1880s, precisely the period when public interest regulation and the rule of reasonableness were flourishing. Between 1860 and 1938 there were years when trade association activity declined, but the general trend was upward. The decline in the rate of organization during the early 1920s is probably best explained by the rapid expansion of the economy in a climate of relative laissez faire, and the decline during the Great Depression most likely reflects general unemployment in both productive and transfer activity.

Despite these post–World War I fluctuations, however, by 1938 trade associations had a substantial command over resources. In that year total income of associations was $70 million, or an average of $48,000.[27] It is not insignificant that between 1920 and 1938 trade associations were organized more frequently in industries where government regulation was greatest. Of the associations in existence in 1938, 61 percent of those in mining, manufacturing, and construction; 57 percent in fisheries; 55 percent in service trades; 49 percent in transportation, communication, and other public utilities; and 46 percent in finance and real estate were organized after 1920.[28]

Although these data suggest that trade associations grew in importance after the Civil War, it would be incorrect and unfair to imply that all association activity was aimed at transfers. Table 4 shows the various activities of associations in 1938, ranked by the frequency with which they were reported as being of major importance. Like farm organizations, associations performed productive services for their members and for society including the collection and distribution of statistics, market surveys, and the coordination of research and development efforts. On the other hand, these same associations offered an excellent example of what Adam Smith meant when he said, "People of the same trade seldom meet together, even for merriment and diversion, but the conversation ends in a conspiracy against the public, or in some contrivance to raise prices."[29] Illegal restraints of trade designed to transfer wealth to members and away from nonmembers were not uncommon. These clearly constituted negative-sum games. But the legalized restraints on competition were just as negative sum as the illegal activities.[30]

Of the many activities of trade associations, however, one of the most important was the "joint representation before legislative and administrative agencies,"[31] or government relations. In the 1938 survey of trade associations conducted by the Temporary National Economic Committee, of all activities undertaken by associations, government relations continually ranked as the most important. This included gathering information for government bodies; acting as industry representatives to legislative bodies, tariff and trade agreement agencies, taxation agencies, scientific or technical agencies, and other executive or administrative agencies; reporting governmental activities; and drafting and promoting model laws. Over 60 percent of the associations were engaged in reporting to governmental bodies or acting as industry representatives to legislative bodies or to other executive or administra-

TABLE 4

RANKING OF TRADE ASSOCIATION ACTIVITIES, 1938

	Rank by frequency with which reported as of major importance	Rank by total frequency with which reported		Rank by frequency with which reported as of major importance	Rank by total frequency with which reported
Government relations	1	1	Public relations	11	9
Trade promotion	2	2	Accounting, cost statistics and studies	12	10
Standardization and simplification	3	6	Credit information service	13	14
Conventions	4	8	Traffic and transportation	14	13
Trade practices	5	3	Price and bid information	15	16
Trade statistics	6	11	Commercial arbitration	16	15
Employer-employee relations	7	5	Collection service	17	17
Miscellaneous services	8	4	Registration of patents, trademarks, designs, and styles	18	18
Statistical republications and special studies	9	7			
Technical research and advisory services	10	12			

SOURCE: Based on Temporary National Economic Committee, *Trade Association Survey*, prepared by Charles Albert Pearce, Monograph no. 18 (Washington, D.C.: Government Printing Office, 1941), p. 26.

tive agencies. Eighty-two percent of all associations in 1938 engaged in
government relations, and nearly 60 percent considered this function of
major importance. Again for many industries (mining; petroleum production and refining; fishing; finance and real estate; transportation,
communication, and other public utilities; and several others), government relations was the most often reported major activity. In all but 2 of
the 27 industrial categories, government relations was included among
the top five activities. When members were asked in which activity
associations made a "significant contribution," government relations
again topped the list. Even in the cases of associations that disbanded
before 1938, the survey concluded that "many of these industries have
maintained the framework of their associations in order to meet promptly
any emergencies requiring industry action, and particularly, as was emphasized in the replies, to meet demands that may be imposed by the
Government for action on an industry-wide basis."[32]

Data from the trade association survey do not allow a detailed
accounting of resources devoted to transfer activity, legal or illegal. Two
conclusions, however, are clear. From the time we have hypothesized as
the beginning of the transfer society, trade association activity increased.
As James Willard Hurst puts it, people joined in groups "exercising their
freedom to enlist with others and using law positively to mobilize group
power in behalf of individual status."[33] The second conclusion is perhaps
best expressed by Sidney Anderson in his remarks to the 1936 annual
convention of the American Trade Association Executives: "There is no
field in which industry expects, or gets more from its associations than in
that of relations with governmental bodies. This becomes more true year
by year, as government, and particularly the Federal government, plays
an ever-increasing part in our business and industrial life."[34] Transfer
activity was definitely part of association practices—most likely a major
part. In addition to government relations, there were efforts to influence
trade practies, employer-employee relations, and public relations. Each
of these encompassed a degree of transfer activity. In a section of the
Temporary National Economic Committee report entitled "Legalized
Restraint of Competition," Clair Wilcox details the ways trade associations
have molded the law in their behalf: "In several trades where sellers are
numerous the imposition of restraints upon competitive activity has been
authorized by laws enacted by the Congress of the United States and by
the legislatures of the several States." In the case of trucking, Wilcox
concludes that "in the railway industry, it was the original purpose of

regulation to prevent monopolistic price increases by establishing maximum rates. In the trucking industry, it is the apparent purpose of regulation to prevent competitive price reduction by establishing minimum rates."[35] Perhaps Adam Smith's words quoted earlier should be amended to read: "People of trade *and government* seldom meet together but the conversation ends in a conspiracy against the public or in some contrivance to raise prices." To the extent that trade association activity was representative of other group and individual efforts, the U.S. economy before World War II can safely be categorized as a transfer society.

Experience during and since World War II leaves little doubt that the importance of transfers has continued to grow. But even for this more recent period, consistent time series data on the extent of transfer activity do not exist. With the growing interest in regulation and political economy in general, however, there have been many industry-specific studies that suggest the value of obtaining rights through the transfer process and therefore serve as evidence of transfer activity.

Trucking is an industry where regulation has generated economic rents. All interstate trucking is regulated by the Interstate Commerce Commission, but the household goods portion has recently received some extensive examination. If Wilcox is correct in asserting that the trucking industry is able "to prevent competitive price reductions by establishing minimum rates," interstate moving rates should be higher than *unregulated* intrastate rates. Table 5 compares intrastate and interstate moving costs and reveals the significance of the difference. The actions of the Interstate Commerce Commission have enabled holders of the moving certificates allotted to a limited number of companies to obtain rates of return above competitive rates. The value of these certificates should reflect the capitalized value to the monopoly returns. In an article, "The Monopoly Value of Household-Goods Carrier Operating Certificates," Dennis Breen estimates that the discounted value of the fourteen nationwide certificates issued by the ICC is between $10 million and $32 million.[36] Combining this with the less-than-nationwide certificates valued at $29 million brings the aggregate to between $39 million and $61 million. Thomas Moore estimates that for the top two revenue classes of all shippers in 1972 "the value of certificates and permits outstanding . . . were worth between $2.1 billion and $3 billion."[37] Such results lead Breen to conclude that "the estimated monopoly value . . . represents a redistribution of income in favor of the initial owner of certificates. Whether or not this redistribution from

TABLE 5

INTRASTATE AND INTERSTATE MOVING COSTS
(7,000-pound, 125-mile shipment)

	Intrastate Rates (averages)	Interstate Rates	Difference (percentage)
All movers			
From Baltimore			
September 1973	$319	$461	+44.5
March 1974	382	533	+39.5
From Maryland suburbs of Washington, D.C.			
September 1973	351	552	+57.3
March 1974	381	637	+67.2
Interstate movers only			
From Baltimore			
September 1973	$325	$461	+41.8
March 1974	421	533	+26.6
From Maryland suburbs of Washington, D.C.			
September 1973	395	552	+39.7
March 1974	468	637	+36.1

SOURCE: Based on Dennis Breen, "Regulation and Household Moving Costs," *Regulation* (September/October 1978): 53.

consumers to producers is desirable in and of itself is a normative issue."[38] But our point is that it is not normative. Producers and consumers should be willing to spend up to the value of the redistribution to obtain or prevent the transfer. This transfer activity is a negative-sum game because it consumes resources. Compared with the GNP, the $62 million or even the $3 billion may appear insignificant, but one must keep in mind that this is only one industry.

Similar results are found in the case of federal regulations on milk prices:

In the United States there are almost 300,000 dairy farmers, none of whom possess any significant market power. Yet, the markets for raw fluid milk in the United States diverge considerably from what would be expected in a competitive environment. The reason for this divergence is the existence of federal and state regulations that affect prices, outputs, costs, and locations of milk flows throughout the United States. The regulations have existed in some part of the country for over forty years, but the portion of U.S. output which is subject to government regulation has steadily increased. Of the 1.1 billion hundredweight of raw milk sold in the United

States in 1973 (valued at $8 billion), approximately 60 percent was pro-
duced in federally regulated areas; another 15 percent was subject to state
regulation.[39]

The authors of this study conclude that at the federal level alone, the
social cost of milk regulation is between $58 million and $64 million.[40]
Again, one can argue that this simply constitutes a redistribution from
consumers to producers, but to the extent that resources are used in an
effort to obtain the redistribution, the net output of society is reduced.
The estimates of social cost represent upper bounds on the amount
individuals and groups would be willing to spend effecting the transfer.
To the extent that there is competition in the transfer arena, all of these
economic rents are dissipated.[41]

Limitations on entry into the medical, dental, and legal professions
have also generated economic returns above a competitive level. It is
estimated that the competitive-equilibrium number of lawyers in 1970
was nearly 20 percent above the actual number and that the differential
has been growing since the 1950s.[42] The result is that actual earnings in
1970 were nearly 30 percent above equilibrium. Empirical estimates of
the impact of licensing restrictions on the cost of dental care suggest that
"the price of dental services and mean dentist income are between 12
and 15 percent higher in nonreciprocity jurisdictions when other factors
are accounted for. Overall, the annual cost of this form of professional
control is approximately $700 million."[43] Our point is that such restric-
tions constitute transfers that wealth maximizers will invest resources to
obtain. Since most of the restrictions result from entry limitations into
professional schools, students invest considerable resources trying to
gain admittance. Although these activities may improve the quality of
professional services, it is questionable whether their marginal impact on
quality is large. To the extent that these are valuable resources invested
to obtain a transfer from consumers to producers, they again are
negative sum. Lawrence Shepard concludes from his study of dental care
that "pending proposals for licensure reform could eliminate these costs
while effecting a more efficient geographical distribution of dentists.
These conclusions may have broader applicability given the large
number of occupational groups that control the competitive environment
in which they operate through state licensing boards."[44]

The range of empirical estimates of transfer activity is broad and
continues to grow. From forestry to fishing, from airlines to trucking,

and from welfare programs to political campaigns, the evidence is clear: we do invest considerable resources in transfer activity. Other wealth-using activities for which no empirical estimates have been made abound in our society. High marginal tax rates cause individuals to substitute leisure for work. Barter, an extremely inefficient market mechanism, becomes more prevalent. Many investment decisions are based on their impact on the taxpayer's tax liability rather than on their pretax rate of return. Inefficient and unwieldly forms of economic organizations exist because they shield assets from income and inheritance taxes. A complete statistical test of our arguments must await further research, but the correlation between the degree of transfer activity since the Civil War and changes in Supreme Court interpretations of the Constitution makes it clear that private rights are not nearly as secure as they once were. The contract clause, the commerce clause, and the due process amendments have all been used to encourage wealth accumulation through negative-sum games. We do live in a transfer society, and the evidence presented above suggests that that society is growing.

NINE
←——————→

Returning to the Contract

Throughout this book we have argued that the last 200 years have witnessed a significant transformation in the rules governing economic activities in the United States. The Founding Fathers had a particular vision about the nature of a "good society." They recognized that there was a protective and a productive role for government in their society. But their vision of government, the holder of the legal monopoly on coercion, also included severe constraints on its ability to use that coercion. The Constitution was the higher rule of law that was to provide those constraints. We have used the productive/transfer activity dichotomy to discuss the original constraints on government and the substantial alterations that have occurred in these constraints. Using this classification, we found that transfer activity, originally quite limited, has come to play a much more significant role in the lives of all Americans. The case-by-case review of the changes discussed in the previous chapters reveals that each had its merits. The protective and productive roles envisioned in the Constitution also provided a means for rationalizing many rule changes. Case after case came before the courts challenging the constitutionality of transfer activity. Not surprisingly, some courts were eventually convinced that this activity was appropriate for government. The distinction between the protective/productive functions of the state and transfer activity is sometimes difficult to make. Two centuries of interpretation, however, have eliminated whatever distinction that once existed. The results of this piecemeal approach have been self-supporting and cumulative to the point where we now have what James Buchanan refers to as "constitutional anarchy."[1] In the words of Herbert Stein, former chairman of the Council of Economic Advisers, "no one can imagine the court finding anything in the economic field unconstitutional."[2] Incrementalism has led us down the path to the transfer society. Although given the current set of institutions it makes sense for individuals to engage in transfer activity, we as a society are made worse off by such endeavors. In fact, it may well be that there are *no* net gainers in the transfer society. The size of the pie may be reduced so much by individuals using resources to obtain and prevent transfers of rights that, no matter how big a slice one ends up with, all slices would be larger if resources flowed instead to productive activity. Although the verification of this conjecture continues to be the subject of much economic research, it does seem clear that our economy is operating at a level below its productive potential and that there would be net gains from a movement away from the transfer society. If this is true, why does such a movement not take place?

There are at least two possible answers to this question. The first argues that the people and groups in our society who have a comparative advantage at transfer activity benefit substantially from the transfer process. For these people any move toward a productive society would result in a loss. Most studies of regulated sectors show that large profits at the expense of the consumers accrue to those who are regulated. These gainers have mastered the transfer game and therefore oppose any reduction in the transfer society. One need only suggest deregulation or relaxation of tariff barriers to arouse opposition. For groups or individuals deriving their wealth from transfers, a move in the direction of productive activity would put them at a comparative disadvantage.

There are two problems with this explanation. First, it is difficult to find anyone who does not gain from transfer activity. All of us are members of some special interest group. The group may have been formed for productive purposes or for transfer prevention, but with the transfer door wide open none can resist increasing individual wealth through this mechanism. Second, this explanation suggests that transfer activity could be reduced by reducing the power of certain groups. Our characterization of the wealth-maximizing process, however, argues that as long as transfers are available, individuals will seek them. If one group loses its comparative advantage at transfer activity, another will take its place. To think that a limited number of vested interests are responsible for preventing any serious attempts at dismantling the transfer society lulls us into believing that the solution to the problem is a simple one, requiring only that those interests be stripped of their power.

The second explanation does not depend on the relative strengths of interest groups. We can call this explanation for the continued growth of transfers the "you first" or the "after you" syndrome. Since the transfer society has grown to such proportions that nearly everyone benefits from the process, it would be difficult to dismantle the system piecemeal. It might be compared to a gunfight in which two parties have weapons aimed at one another. Each agrees to put down his gun if the other does so first. The one who first relinquishes the self-protection benefits will bear significant costs if the other does not follow the agreement. Similarly in the transfer society, even if we all recognize the desirability of limiting transfer activity, each of us is reluctant to start the process. All have an incentive to say, "I will stop engaging in transfer activity if you stop first." But no one has the incentive to be the first. Of course, we will attempt to reduce the transfer activity from which others benefit, but since the benefits of transfer activity tend to be concentrated and the costs diffuse, these attempts are unlikely to receive widespread support. As Ralph Winter, Jr., puts it, "What voters *may* instinctively understand is that the elimination of programs which significantly benefit them will reduce taxes and government *only* when combined with a number of others which do not."[3] Because of the concentrated benefits and diffuse costs, transfer activity is difficult to stop. Unfortunately, the process is like a ratchet, making it impossible for us to return to a productive society through incremental changes. Incrementalism may have led us to the transfer society, but it is unlikely to lead us away from it.

Given the difficulty of limiting transfers by incremental alterations in the law, it appears that only more fundamental changes have any hope of succeeding. In this work we have concentrated on the Constitution because we see it as the most basic source of limits on transfer activity in the past. Likewise, only through constitutional reform is there any hope of significantly constraining transfers in the future. Rather than "you first," it must be "all together now." Madison said that "in framing a government . . . the great difficulty lies in this: you must first enable the government to control the governed; and in the next place oblige it to control itself."[4] In our minds the efforts to accomplish the latter task were partially successful; for a period of time the government was controlled. However, in view of the present state of affairs, we believe that a "constitutional revolution" as called for by James Buchanan[5] is a necessary precondition for regaining a world in which productive

endeavors dominate transfer endeavors. This historical study has illumi-
nated some of the areas where the contract should be strengthened. We
do not know whether the constitutional revolution will or should take
place through amendments or through a general rewriting of the
document. Whatever the process, however, it is essential that the concept
of a government limited by a set of fundamental, difficult-to-change
rules dominate our thinking.

This brings us to the two major conclusions of our book: the necessity
of basic rules to limit wasteful transfer activity and the importance of
ideas regarding limits on government. A formal agreement on the
fundamental rights of the members of society is essential to an orderly,
productive society. Rights must be well defined and enforced if individuals are to interact in positive-sum games. This study has shown,
however, that the existence of fundamental rules is not sufficient to
guarantee domination by productive activity. The United States began
with a set of fundamental rules that promoted this activity, but changing
ideas regarding limits on government slowly eroded these rules. Only if
members of society understand and believe in the distinct difference
between the constitutional contract and the day-to-day operating rules of
the society (the law) is there any hope of maintaining agreed limits on
transfer activity. A people's concept of the appropriate role of the
coercive powers of government is crucially important in determining the
path society takes. Ideas do matter. In conclusion, therefore, we call for
two major social transformations: an intellectual revolution strengthening
our ideological commitment to basic rules limiting transfer activity and a
constitutional revolution embodying that commitment.

Notes

CHAPTER TWO

1. Buchanan (1975), p. 2.

2. Again the reader is urged to remember that we define positive-sum games strictly in terms of increased total output or movements of resources from lower- to higher-valued alternatives. We make no allowance for interpersonal utility comparisons.

3. For a summary of the property rights literature, see Furubotn and Pejovich (1972).

4. To the extent that these efforts are designed to establish exclusivity over unclaimed resources, they produce an institution, private property, that encourages the productive activity described in the text. To be sure, resources are used in the process, but these resources are the cost of producing the institution. The American West provides an excellent example of this type of activity; see Anderson and Hill (1975).

5. Tullock (1971), p. 642.

6. There is of course an optimal level of law enforcement based on the additional benefits and costs of such enforcement. For a discussion of this, see Becker (1968).

7. With nonexclusivity, rents to resources become an uncaptured residual that decision units will expend efforts trying to obtain. For a discussion of this type of rent dissipation, see Cheung (1970).

8. One can argue that public employees may gain positive utility from the transfer activity and such waste is thus reduced. That is, the bureaucrat in charge of handing out special favors (rights) may derive satisfaction from the transfer activity. We do not include that utility in our measure of social product when we say that transfer activity is wasteful.

9. The potential that the state will use its coercive power illegitimately always exists. Providing effective limits on the government's legal monopoly on coercion is difficult at best. We discuss, in the context of transfers, why it has been difficult in the American case to limit government power. We do not, however, attempt to provide a detailed treatment of the more general issue of limiting government.

10. A third reason is often suggested. Knowledge of how involuntary transfers can increase the total utility in society because the utility lost by those from whom rights are transferred is less than the utility gained by those to whom rights are transferred could justify such transfers. We do not treat this possibility.

11. For a discussion of the legitimacy of constitutional contracts, see Buchanan (1975), pp. 83–85, and Scott Gordon's (1976) discussion of Buchanan's legitimacy criteria.

12. Of course there are problems inherent in this approach aside from the ones treated in the text. A major one is that such action by the state assumes that a measurement can be made by the state of the worth of such a dam to downstream users and that those users can be taxed accordingly.

13. Buchanan (1975) makes clear the limits of this productive role. We emphasize that coercion "may be" necessary since there is some evidence that the public goods argument has been misused; see Coase (1974) and Anderson and Hill (1979).

14. Johnson (1973), p. 305.

15. For a discussion of this capture process with respect to railroads, see Kolko (1965).

16. North (1979), pp. 256–57.

17. Buchanan (1975), p. 53.

CHAPTER THREE

1. Anderson (1975).

2. North (1974), p. 48.

3. North and Thomas (1973).

4. For a discussion of the impact of changing factor endowments of the terms of the contract, see Anderson and Reed (1973).

5. Previté-Orton (1952), p. 425.

6. North and Thomas (1973), p. 11.

7. Holt (1965), pp. 1–18.

8. Corwin (1928), pp. 31–54.

9. For a discussion of this change, see Tollison (1978).

10. Chrimes (1965), pp. 100–120.

11. North and Thomas (1973), p. 156.

12. Locke's major work is *Two Treatises of Government* (1965).

13. Locke (1965), p. 309.

14. A major area of difficulty for modern interpreters of Locke has been his emphasis on both majority rule and the supremacy of individual property

rights. What happens when a majority decides to remove the property of a member of the society is not at all clear.

15. North and Thomas (1973), p. 18.
16. See, for example, Thomas (1965) and (1968).
17. Bailyn (1967), p. 94.
18. Ibid., p. 99.
19. Bailyn (1976).
20. Bailyn (1973), pp. 26—27.
21. Ibid., p. 12.
22. Wood (1969), pp. 12—13.
23. Diamond (1975).
24. Paine (1969), pp. 30—31.

CHAPTER FOUR

1. Hughes, (1976a).
2. For a detailed discussion of the political economy of the era, see Wood (1969) and Johnson (1973).
3. Sullivan (1792), pp. 5—6.
4. Johnson (1973), p. 24.
5. Kristol (1975), p. 42; see also Spengler (1940), p. 10.
6. Webster (1785), p. 6.
7. Quoted in Mudge (1939), p. 12.
8. Taylor (1814), p. 634.
9. Johnson (1973), p. 63.
10. Mudge (1939), p. 15.
11. Madison, *The Federalist 37*.
12. Madison, *The Federalist 51*.
13. Madison, *The Federalist 10*.
14. Hamilton, *The Federalist 6*.
15. Madison, *The Federalist 51*.
16. Madison, *The Federalist 53*.
17. Hamilton, *The Federalist 78*.
18. Madison, *The Federalist 49*.
19. Madison, *The Federalist 10*.
20. Ibid.
21. Madison, *The Federalist 62*.
22. Main (1961), p. 150.
23. Madison, *The Federalist 10*.

24. Quoted in Wood (1969), p. 460.

25. Kelly and Harbison (1970), p. 106.

26. Madison, *The Federalist 44*.

27. Madison, *The Federalist 51*.

28. For a more detailed discussion of the role of the federal judiciary, see Kelly and Harbison (1970), pp. 136–47.

29. Ibid., p. 165.

30. Buchanan (1975), p. 77.

31. Hamilton, *The Federalist 7*.

32. Madison, *The Federalist 44*.

33. As is discussed below, this clause was eventually construed to imply positive power for the purpose of regulation by the central government.

34. Madison, *The Federalist 42*.

35. Ackerman (1977), pp. 7–8.

CHAPTER FIVE

1. Kelly and Harbison (1970), p. 173.

2. Quoted in Konefsky (1964), pp. 250–51.

3. Quoted in Baker (1974), p. 368.

4. Quoted in Konefsky (1964), p. 91.

5. E. Warren (1956), p. xv.

6. Baker (1974), p. 654.

7. 6 Cranch 135 (1810).

8. Konefsky (1964), p. 130.

9. Quoted in ibid., pp. 148–49.

10. 4 Wheaton 627 (1819).

11. 4 Wheaton 198 (1819).

12. McMillan v. McNeill, 4 Wheaton 212–18 (1819).

13. McMillan v. McNeill, 4 Wheaton 213 (1819).

14. 12 Wheaton 339 (1827).

15. 12 Wheaton 346 (1827).

16. 12 Wheaton 354–55 (1827).

17. Wright (1938), p. 50.

18. 4 Wheaton 427 (1819).

19. Quoted in Konefsky (1964), p. 186.

20. Higgs (1971), p. 55.

21. For an excellent discussion of the continued presence of government, see Hughes (1977).

22. Johnson (1973), p. 200.

23. For a discussion of arguments surrounding tariff laws, see Edwards (1970).

24. Davis et al. (1972), p. 497.

25. Even if one argues that subsidies to social overhead capital are necessary to equate private and social rates of return, once the mechanism to use coercion is established it is difficult to limit use of that coercion.

26. Friedman (1973), p. 157.

27. Johnson (1973), p. 162.

28. See Handlin and Handlin (1969), Hartz (1948), Horwitz (1977), and Friedman (1973) for various examples of this type of state regulation.

29. For example, see Scheiber (1971).

30. Scheiber (1975) discusses the unwillingness of states to use the full potential of their regulatory power because of fear of what other states might do.

31. Friedman (1973), p. 163. Jonathan R. T. Hughes makes the same point: "There was not much nonmarket control at the Federal level in 1861" (Hughes [1976b], p. 60).

32. Scheiber (1973), p. 243.

33. Horwitz (1976), p. 255.

34. Hurst (1964), p. 3.

35. Quoted in Johnson (1973), p. 170.

36. Quoted in ibid., p. 172.

37. Baker (1974), p. 667.

CHAPTER SIX

1. Kelly and Harbison (1970), pp. 325–26.

2. C. Warren (1937), p. 33.

3. 11 Peters 420 (1837).

4. Providence Bank v. Billings, 4 Peters 560 (1830).

5. Kelly and Harbison (1970), p. 346.

6. Wright (1938), p. 63.

7. U.S., Bureau of the Census (1975), p. 8.

8. Lebergott (1966), p. 118.

9. Blau (1954), pp. 32–33.

10. Madison, *The Federalist 51*.

11. Williamson (1960), pp. 243–45.

12. See, for example, Davies (1954), pp. 38–53, and Leggett (1954), pp. 66–88.

13. For this argument, see Beard (1913).

14. For a discussion of the impact of democracy on the growth of government, see Meltzer and Richard (1978), pp. 111—18.

15. Robinson (1954), p. 325.

16. Skidmore (1954), p. 356.

CHAPTER SEVEN

1. For a discussion of how the emancipation of the slaves was simply a delayed fulfillment of the ideology of the Declaration of Independence *and* the Constitution, see Jaffa (1978).

2. Hurst (1964), p. 76.

3. Ibid.

4. Gray and Peterson (1974), p. 273.

5. Lindert and Williamson (1976), p. 102.

6. Ibid., pp. 89—90.

7. Gray and Peterson (1974), p. 288.

8. North (1974), pp. 152—53.

9. See McGee (1958).

10. See Higgs (1970).

11. Friedman (1973), p. 296.

12. Gray and Peterson (1974), p. 269.

13. Hughes (1976a).

14. Scheiber (1971).

15. Hughes (1976b), pp. 62, 52.

16. Twiss (1942), p. 63.

17. Ibid.

18. Wells (1874), pp. 282—83.

19. Cary (1875), p. 10.

20. *First Annual Report of Railroad Commissioners of State of Wisconsin, 1874*, p. 64; quoted in Twiss (1942), p. 68.

21. Cary (1875), p. 64.

22. Goudy (1875), p. 1.

23. Ibid., p. 21.

24. Twiss (1942), pp. 83—84.

25. *Chicago Tribune*, March 3, 1877.

26. "The Potter Act at Washington," *American Law Review* 9 (1875): 235.

27. 94 U.S. 126 (1877).

28. It is not clear whether those in the majority regarded their decision as breaking new constitutional ground. A case could have been made for regulating grain storage rates as an extension of the government's right to regulate

common carriers. The opinion did not do that and the ambiguous phrase "affected with a public interest" did become a rationale for regulating all economic activity. For a discussion of this issue, see Kitch and Bowler (1978).

29. 94 U.S. 140 (1877).

30. 94 U.S. 143 (1877).

31. 94 U.S. 152 (1877).

32. 94 U.S. 186 (1877).

33. 143 U.S. 517 (1892).

34. *St. Paul Pioneer Press*, March 13, 1877.

35. *New York Times*, March 29, 1877.

36. Goudy (1875), pp. 50—51.

37. See Corwin (1941), p. 29.

38. Kelly and Harbison (1970), p. 527.

39. Holden v. Hardy, 169 U.S. 366 (1898), and Lochner v. New York, 198 U.S. 45 (1905).

40. Loan Association v. Topeka, 20 Wallace 655 (1875).

41. Field v. Clark, 143 U.S. 649 (1892); Buttfield v. Stranahan, 192 U.S. 470 (1904); and United States v. Grimaud, 220 U.S. 506 (1911).

42. For an excellent review of this type of behavior aimed at securing political positions, see Glasscock (1935).

43. For a lengthier discussion of this transfer activity in conjunction with due process, see Kelly and Harbison (1970), pp. 501—24.

CHAPTER EIGHT

1. Schlesinger (1973).

2. Hughes (1977).

3. Ibid., pp. 133—34.

4. Ibid., p. 135.

5. Kelly and Harbison (1970), pp. 714—18.

6. Ibid., p. 736.

7. Ibid., p. 738.

8. 291 U.S. 537 (1934).

9. Kelly and Harbison (1970), p. 793.

10. Brittan (1978).

11. Ibid., p. 246.

12. Ibid., p. 265.

13. Ibid., pp. 265—66.

14. Krueger (1974), p. 294.

15. Kraus (1979), p. 16.

16. Bartley (1979), p. 24.
17. Feige (1979).
18. Meltzer and Richard (1978), p. 111.
19. Ibid., p. 115.
20. Friedman (1973), pp. 296–97.
21. Hurst (1964), p. 85.
22. Gardner (1949), p. 91.
23. Ibid.
24. Ibid., p. 94.
25. Ibid., p. 100.
26. Davis and North (1971), p. 100.
27. Temporary National Economic Committee (1941), p. 7.
28. Ibid., p. 12.
29. Smith (1937), p. 128.
30. For a general discussion, see Temporary National Economic Committee (1940), pp. 267–79.
31. Ibid., p. 226.
32. Temporary National Economic Committee (1941), p. 19.
33. Hurst (1964), p. 86.
34. Quoted in Temporary National Economic Committee (1941), p. 335.
35. Temporary National Economic Committee (1940), pp. 267–68.
36. Breen (1977), p. 177.
37. Moore (1978), p. 342.
38. Breen (1977), p. 180.
39. Ippolito and Masson (1978), p. 33.
40. Ibid., p. 60.
41. For a discussion of rent dissipation, see Cheung (1970).
42. Pashigian (1977), p. 75.
43. Shepard (1978), p. 200. Nonreciprocity jurisdictions are those that do not honor licenses from other states and thereby control market entry.
44. Ibid., pp. 200–201.

CHAPTER NINE

1. Buchanan (1975), p. 14.
2. Stein (1974).
3. Winter (1978), p. 12.
4. Madison, *The Federalist 51.*
5. Buchanan (1975), chapter 10.

Bibliography

Ackerman, Bruce A. *Private Property and the Constitution.* New Haven and London: Yale University Press, 1977.

Anderson, Terry L. "Wealth Estimates for the New England Colonies, 1650–1709." *Explorations in Economic History* 12, no. 2 (April 1975): 151–76.

Anderson, Terry L., and Hill, Peter J. "The Evolution of Property Rights: A Study of the American West." *Journal of Law and Economics* 18, no. 1 (April 1975): 163–79.

———. "An American Experiment in Anarcho-Capitalism: The Not So Wild, Wild West." *Journal of Libertarian Studies* 3, no. 1 (1979): 9–30.

Anderson, Terry L., and Reed, Clyde. "An Economic Explanation of Twelfth- and Thirteenth-Century English Agricultural Organization." *Economic History Review* 2d series, 26, no. 1 (February 1973): 134–37.

Bailyn, Bernard. *The Ideological Origins of the American Revolution.* Cambridge, Mass.: Harvard University Press, Belknap Press, 1967.

———. "The Central Themes of the American Revolution: An Interpretation." In Stephen G. Kurtz and James H. Huston, eds., *Essays on the American Revolution.* Chapel Hill: University of North Carolina Press, 1973.

———. "1776: A Year of Challenge—A World Transformed." *Journal of Law and Economics* 19, no. 3 (October, 1976): 437–66.

Baker, Leonard. *John Marshall: A Life in Law.* New York: Macmillan Company, 1974.

Bartley, Robert L. "Sweden Faces a Cloudy Future." *Wall Street Journal,* February 21, 1979.

Beard, Charles A. *An Economic Interpretation of the Constitution of the United States.* New York: Macmillan Company, 1913.

Becker, Gary S. "Crime and Punishment: An Economic Approach." *Journal of Political Economy* 76 (March/April 1968): 169–217.

Blau, Joseph, ed. *Social Theories of Jacksonian Democracy.* New York: Liberal Arts Press, 1954.

Breen, Dennis A. "The Monopoly Value of Household-Goods Carrier Operating Certificates." *Journal of Law and Economics* 20, no. 1 (April 1977): 153–85.

———. "Regulation and Household Moving Costs." *Regulation* (September/ October, 1978): 51–54.

Brittan, Samuel. "How British is the British Sickness?" *Journal of Law and Economics* 21, no. 2 (October 1978): 245–68.

Buchanan, James. *The Limits of Liberty*. Chicago: University of Chicago Press, 1975.

———. *Freedom in Constitutional Contract*. College Station: Texas A & M University Press, 1977.

Cary, J. W. *Peik* v. *Chicago and Northwestern Railway Company: Brief for Appellants*. Illinois Supreme Court (October term, 1875).

Cheung, Steven N. S. "The Structure of a Contract and the Theory of a Nonexclusive Resource." *Journal of Law and Economics*, 13, no. 1 (April 1970): 49–70.

Chrimes, S. B. *English Constitutional History*. London: Oxford University Press, 1965.

Coase, Ronald. "The Lighthouse in Economics." *Journal of Law and Economics* 17, no. 2 (October 1974): 357–76.

Corwin, Edward S. *The "Higher Law" Background of American Constitutional Law*. Ithaca, N.Y.: Cornell University Press, 1928.

———. *Constitutional Revolution, Ltd*. Claremont, Calif.: Claremont Colleges, 1941.

Davies, Charles Steward. "Popular Government." In Joseph Blau, ed., *Social Theories of Jacksonian Democracy*. New York: Liberal Arts Press, 1954.

Davis, Lance E.; Easterlin, Richard A.; and Parker, William N.; et al. *American Economic Growth: An Economists' History of the United States*. New York: Harper & Row, 1972.

Davis, Lance E., and North, Douglass C. *Institutional Change and American Economic Growth*. London: Cambridge University Press, 1971.

Diamond, Martin. "The Revolution of Sober Expectations." In *The American Revolution: Three Views*. New York: American Brands, 1975.

Edwards, Richard. "Economic Sophistication in Nineteenth-Century Congressional Tariff Debates." *Journal of Economic History* 30 (December 1970): 802–28.

Feige, Edgar L. "How Big Is the Irregular Economy?" *Challenge*, November/ December 1979, pp. 5–13.

Friedman, Lawrence M. *A History of American Law*. New York: Simon & Schuster, 1973.

Furubotn, Eirik G., and Pejovich, Svetozar. "Property Rights and Economic Theory: A Survey of Recent Literature." *Journal of Economic Literature* 10, no. 4 (1972): 1137–162.

Gardner, Charles M. *The Grange—Friend of the Farmer*. Washington, D.C: National Grange, 1949.

Glasscock, Carl Burgess. *The War of the Copper Kings.* New York: Bobbs-Merrill, 1935.

Gordon, H. Scott. "The New Contractarians." *Journal of Political Economy* 84 (June 1976): 573–90.

Goudy, W. C. *Munn and Scott* v. *Illinois: Brief and Argument for Plaintiffs in Error.* Illinois Supreme Court (October term, 1875).

Gray, Ralph, and Peterson, John M. *Economic Development of the United States.* Homewood, Ill.: Irwin, 1974.

Hamilton, Alexander; Madison, James; and Jay, John. *The Federalist Papers.* New York: New American Library, 1961.

Handlin, Oscar, and Handlin, Mary. *Commonwealth: A Study of the Role of Government in the American Economy, Massachusetts, 1774–1861.* Cambridge, Mass.: Harvard University Press, 1969.

Hartz, Louis, *Economic Policy and Democratic Thought: Pennsylvania, 1776–1869.* Cambridge, Mass.: Harvard University Press, 1948.

Higgs, Robert. "Railroad Rates and the Populist Uprising." *Agriculture History* 44 (July 1970): 291–97.

———. *The Transformation of the American Economy, 1865–1914.* New York: John Wiley & Sons, 1971.

Holt, J. C. *Magna Carta.* London: Cambridge University Press, 1965.

Horwitz, Morton J. "The Legacy of 1776 in Legal and Economic Thought." *Journal of Law and Economics* 19, no. 3 (October 1976): 621–32.

———. *The Transformation of American Law, 1780–1860.* Cambridge, Mass.: Harvard University Press, 1977.

Hughes, Jonathan R. T. *Social Control in the Colonial Economy.* Charlottesville: University Press of Virginia, 1976a.

———. "Transference and Development of Institutional Constraints Upon Economic Activity." In Paul Uselding, ed., *Research in Economic History*, vol. 1. Greenwich Conn.: JAI Press, 1976b.

———. *The Governmental Habit: Economic Controls from Colonial Times to the Present.* New York: Basic Books, 1977.

Hurst, James Willard. *Laws and the Conditions of Freedom in the Nineteenth-Century United States.* Madison: University of Wisconsin Press, 1964.

Ippolito, Richard A., and Masson, Robert T. "The Social Cost of Government Regulation of Milk." *Journal of Law and Economics* 21, no. 1 (April 1978): 33–65.

Jaffa, Harry V. *How to Think About The American Revolution.* Durham, N.C.: Carolina Academic Press, 1978.

Johnson, E. A. J. *The Foundations of American Economic Freedom.* Minneapolis: University of Minnesota Press, 1973.

Kelly, Alfred H., and Harbison, Winfred A. *The American Constitution*, 4th ed. New York: W. W. Norton & Company, 1970.

Kile, Orville Merton. *The Farm Bureau Through Three Decades*. Baltimore: Waverly Press, 1948.

Kitch, Edmund W., and Bowler, Clara Ann. "The Facts of Munn v. Illinois." *Supreme Court Review* 1978.

Kolko, Gabriel. *Railroads and Regulation: 1877–1916*. Princeton, N.J.: Princeton University Press, 1965.

Konefsky, Samuel J. *John Marshall and Alexander Hamilton: Architects of the American Constitution*. New York: Macmillan Company, 1964.

Kraus, Melvin. "The Swedish Tax Revolt." *Wall Street Journal*, February 1, 1979.

Kristol, Irving. "The American Revolution as a Successful Revolution." In *The American Revolution: Three Views*. New York: American Brands, 1975.

Krueger, Anne O. "The Political Economy of the Rent-Seeking Society." *American Economic Review* 65 (June 1974): 291–303.

Lebergott, Stanley. "Labor Force and Employment, 1800–1960." In *Output, Employment, and Productivity in the United States after 1800*. New York: National Bureau of Economic Research, 1966.

Leggett, William. "Democratic Editorials." In Joseph Blau, ed., *Social Theories of Jacksonian Democracy*. New York: Liberal Arts Press, 1954.

Lindert, Peter H., and Williamson, Jeffrey G. "Three Centuries of American Inequality." In Paul Uselding, ed., *Research in Economic History*, vol. 1. Greenwich, Conn.: JAI Press, 1976.

Locke, John. *Two Treatises of Government*. New York: New American Library, 1965.

Madison, James, see under Hamilton, Alexander.

Main, Jackson Turner. *The Anti-Federalists, 1781–1788*. New York: W. W. Norton & Company, 1961.

McGee, John S. "Predatory Price Cutting: The Standard Oil (N.J.) Case." *Journal of Law and Economics* 1, no. 2 (October 1958): 137–69.

Meltzer, Allan H., and Richard, Scott F. "Why Government Grows (and Grows) in a Democracy." *Public Interest* no. 52 (Summer, 1978): 111–18.

Moore, Thomas Gale. "Beneficiaries of Trucking Regulation." *Journal of Law and Economics* 21, no. 2 (October 1978): 327–43.

Mudge, Eugene Tinbroeck. *The Social Philosophy of John Taylor of Caroline*. New York: Columbia University Press, 1939.

North, Douglass C. *Growth and Welfare in the American Past*, 2d ed. Englewood Cliffs, N.J.: Prentice-Hall, 1974.

———. "A Framework for Analyzing the State in Economic History." *Explorations in Economic History* 16, no. 3 (July 1979): 249–59.

North, Douglass C., and Thomas, Robert Paul. *The Rise of the Western World*. London: Cambridge University Press, 1973.

Paine, Thomas. "Common Sense." In Phillip S. Foner, comp. and ed., *The Collected Works of Thomas Paine*. New York: Citadel Press, 1969.

Pashigian, Peter. "The Market for Lawyers: The Determinants of the Demand for and Supply of Lawyers." *Journal of Law and Economics* 20, no. 1 (April 1977): 53–85.

"The Potter Act at Washington." *American Law Review* 9 (1875).

Previté-Orton, Charles William. *The Shorter Cambridge Medieval History*. London: Cambridge University Press, 1952.

Randall, Alan. "Property Rights and Social Microeconomics." *Natural Resources Journal* 15, no. 4 (October 1975): 729–47.

Robinson, Frederick. "A Program for Labor." In Joseph Blau, ed., *Social Theories of Jacksonian Democracy*. New York: Liberal Arts Press, 1954.

Scheiber, Harry. "The Road to Munn: Eminent Domain and the Concept of Public Purpose in the State Courts." *Perspectives in American History* 5 (1971): 329–402.

———. "Property Law, Expropriation, and Resource Allocation by Government: The United States, 1789–1910." *Journal of Economic History* 23, no. 1 (March 1973): 232–51.

———. "Federalism and the Economic Order, 1789–1910." *Law and Society Review* 10, no. 1 (Fall, 1975): 57–118.

Schlesinger, Arthur M., Jr. *The Imperial Presidency*. Boston: Houghton Mifflin Company, 1973.

Shepard, Lawrence. "Licensing Restrictions and the Cost of Dental Care." *Journal of Law and Economics* 21, no. 1 (April 1978).

Skidmore, Thomas. "A Plan for Equalizing Property." In Joseph Blau, ed., *Social Theories of Jacksonian Democracy*. New York: Liberal Arts Press, 1954.

Smith, Adam. *The Wealth of Nations*. New York: Modern Library, 1937.

Spengler, Joseph J. "The Political Economy of Jefferson, Madison, and Adams." In *American Studies in Honor of W. K. Boyd*. Durham, N.C.: Duke University Press, 1940.

Stein, Herbert. "Grounds for Pessimism." *Wall Street Journal*, December 12, 1974.

Sullivan, James. *The Path to Riches: An Inquiry into the Origins and the Use of Money*. Boston, 1792.

Taylor, John. *An Inquiry into the Principles and Policy of the Government of the United States*. Fredericksburg, Va., 1814.

Temporary National Economic Committee. *Competition and Monopoly In American History*, Monograph no. 21. Washington, D.C.: Government Printing Office, 1940.

———. *Trade Association Survey*, prepared by Charles Albert Pearce, Monograph no. 18. Washington, D.C.: Government Printing Office, 1941.

Thomas, Robert Paul. "A Quantitative Approach to the Study of Effects of

British Imperial Policy upon Colonial Welfare: Some Preliminary Findings." *Journal of Economic History,* 25 (December 1965): 615–38.

———. "British Imperial Policy and the Economic Interpretation of the American Revolution." *Journal of Economic History* 28 (September 1968): 436–40.

Tollison, Robert D. "An Historical Note on Regulatory Reform." *Regulation* (November/December 1978): 46–49.

Tullock, Gordon. "Constitutional Mythology." *New Individualist Review,* 3 (Spring, 1965): 13–17.

———. "The Welfare Costs of Tariffs, Monopolies, and Theft." *Western Economic Journal* 5, no. 3 (June 1967): 224–32.

———. "The Cost of Transfers." *Kyklos* 24 (1971): 629–43.

Twiss, Benjamin R. *Lawyers and the Constitution: How Laissez Faire Came to the Supreme Court.* Princeton, N.J.: Russell & Russell, 1942.

U.S., Bureau of the Census. *Historical Statistics of the United States, Colonial Times to 1970,* Bicentennial ed., part 1. Washington, D.C.: Government Printing Office, 1975.

Vedder, Richard K. *The American Economy in Historical Perspective.* Belmont, Calif.: Wadsworth, 1976.

Warren, Charles. *The Supreme Court in United States History.* 2 vols. Boston: Little, Brown and Company, 1937.

Warren, Earl. "Foreword." In W. Melville Jones, ed., *Chief Justice John Marshall: A Reappraisal.* Ithaca: Cornell University Press, 1956.

Webster, Noah. *Sketches of American Policy.* Hartford, 1785.

Wells, David A. "How Will the Supreme Court Decide the Granger Railroad Cases?" *Nation* 19 (1874).

Williamson, Chilton. *American Suffrage: From Property to Democracy, 1760–1860.* Princeton, N.J.: Princeton University Press, 1960.

Winter, Ralph K., Jr. "The Welfare State and the Decline of Electoral Politics." *Regulation* (March/April, 1978): 11–14.

Wood, Gordon S. *The Creation of the American Republic, 1776–1787.* Williamsburg, Va.: University of North Carolina Press and Institute of Early American History and Culture, 1969.

Wright, Benjamin F. *The Contract Clause of the Constitution.* Cambridge, Mass.: Harvard University Press, 1938.

COURT CASES CITED

Adkins v. Children's Hospital, 261 U.S. 525 (1923)
Bronson v. Kinzie, 1 Howard 311 (1843)
Brown v. Maryland, 12 Wheaton 419 (1827)
Budd v. New York, 143 U.S. 517 (1892)
Buttfield v. Stranahan, 192 U.S. 470 (1904)

Champion v. Ames, 188 U.S. 321 (1903)
Champion v. Casey, U.S. Cir. Ct. for Rhode Island (1792)
Charles River Bridge v. Warren Bridge, 11 Peters 420 (1837)
Chicago, Milwaukee & St. Paul Railroad Co. v. Minnesota, 134 U.S. 418 (1890)
Chisholm v. Georgia, 2 Dallas 419 (1793)
Cohens v. Virginia, 6 Wheaton 264 (1821)
Dartmouth College v. Woodward, 4 Wheaton 518 (1819)
Davidson v. New Orleans, 96 U.S. 97 (1878)
Dred Scott v. Sandford, 19 Howard 393 (1857)
Field v. Clark, 143 U.S. 649 (1892)
Fletcher v. Peck, 6 Cranch 87 (1810)
Gibbons v. Ogden, 9 Wheaton 1 (1824)
Hepburn v. Griswold, 8 Wallace 603 (1870)
Holden v. Hardy, 169 U.S. 366 (1898)
Loan Association v. Topeka, 20 Wallace 655 (1875)
Lochner v. New York, 198 U.S. 45 (1905)
Marbury v. Madison, 1 Cranch 137 (1803)
Martin v. Hunter's Lessee, 1 Wheaton 304 (1816)
McCray v. United States, 195 U.S. 27 (1904)
McCulloch v. Maryland, 4 Wheaton 316 (1819)
McMillan v. McNeill, 4 Wheaton 212 (1819)
Muller v. Oregon, 208 U.S. 412 (1908)
Munn v. Illinois, 94 U.S. 113 (1877)
Nebbia v. New York, 291 U.S. 502 (1934)
New York v. Miln, 11 Peters 102 (1837)
N.L.R.B. v. Jones and Laughlin Steel Corporation, 301 U.S. 1 (1937)
Ogden v. Saunders, 12 Wheaton 213 (1827)
Providence Bank v. Billings, 4 Peters 560 (1830)
Slaughterhouse Cases, 16 Wallace 36 (1873)
Stone v. Farmers' Loan and Trust Co., 116 U.S. 307 (1886)
Stone v. Wisconsin, 94 U.S. 186 (1877)
Sturges v. Crowninshield, 4 Wheaton 122 (1819)
Swift and Co. v. United States, 196 U.S. 375 (1905)
Talbot v. Seeman, 1 Cranch 1 (1801)
Trevett v. Weeden, Rhode Island (1786)
United States v. Grimaud, 220 U.S. 506 (1911)
United States v. Peters, 5 Cranch 115 (1809)
United States v. Schooner Peggy, 1 Cranch 103 (1801)
Ware v. Hylton, 3 Dallas 199 (1796)
Wilson v. Mason, 1 Cranch 45 (1801)
Wynehamer v. New York, 13 N.Y. 378 (1856)

Index